D0562583

# The
# LOCAL
# YOLK

THE LOCAL YOLK.
Copyright © 2014 by John Emrich.
All rights reserved.
Printed in the United States of America.
No part of this book may be used or reproduced
without the written permission of the author.

ISBN-13: 9781502400307
ISBN-10: 1502400308

# The
# LOCAL YOLK

Beer, Backyard Chickens, and
The Business of Building a
Sustainable Food System

John Emrich

FOR MY CHILDREN:
Jake, Wade, Kurt and Mack

# Table of Contents

# Preface

"Many people who are going through the early stages of the awakening process are no longer certain what their outer purpose is. What drives the world no longer drives them. Seeing the madness of civilization so clearly, they may feel somewhat alienated from the culture around them. Some feel that they inhabit a no-man's-land between two worlds. They are no longer run by the ego, yet the arising awareness has not yet become fully integrated into their lives. Inner and outer purpose have not merged." – Eckhart Tolle, *A New Earth*

If you spend all day commiserating with like-minded people, it is easy to convince yourself that in some way, everyone shares your views. In the case of a "movement," such as the one towards the expansion of markets for sustainable food, this might mean you come to believe the movement is much larger than it really is. I travel in mixed company, so the delusion doesn't last long. It is a bipolar existence. On any day, the euphoria induced by the consumption of great local food, or by a stroll through a bustling farmers market, inevitably gives way to some depressing news about another victory for agribusiness as usual. Two steps forward and two steps back, and it seems as though we aren't getting anywhere.

But there is change afoot.

The wise among us have stopped paying attention to the negative news. They have turned off their televisions, canceled the newspaper subscriptions, and gotten on with life on their own terms. Like bees that have decided its time to swarm, consumers are unshackling their chains to the industrial food system and choosing a different path. As if on queue, people have stopped reading the books that make their blood boil and decided to build chicken coops and beehives instead. I myself have taken this queue and attempted to write a book that celebrates the *rewards* of the sustainable food movement instead of cataloguing the negative consequences of post-war chemical agriculture. If engaged in the act of persuasion, I've chosen honey over vinegar.

It wasn't easy, and I wasn't always successful. The story of how each individual in this narrative became fully engaged in sustainable agriculture cannot be distilled down to a single variable; each story is more of an equation, the first half of which entails repudiation of a system that, in some way, violated a set of personal values. Some of those details needed to be rehashed. The manuscript was much longer, however, before editing out the diatribes. It is easy, in defense of sustainable food, to get angry. There are plenty of great books that document the horrors of conventional agriculture, from the impact on human and environmental health, to the complicity of large corporations and our own government. Anger, however, is a destructive emotion that consumes the angry and does little to move the dialogue forward.

Mike Callicrate of Ranch Foods Direct is one person who has been through conventional agriculture's emotional meat grinder. Looking back after two decades of fighting the system, he has seen three ways for a food advocate to instigate change. The first two are litigation and legislation. Mike has been the lead plaintiff in a lawsuit against the world's largest meat packing company since the mid-1990's. The litigation is still ongoing (defendants with deep pockets can make that happen), which leads Mike to conclude that litigation obviously hasn't worked. Attempts to change legislation have also failed; the handful of companies that dominate processing and distribution also get to write the rules in Washington D.C. To use the vernacular of the 19th century, industrial food conglomerates are modern-day robber barons that have "seized the narrows" of processing and distribution, allowing them to dictate price and terms to the suppliers, *and* dictate choice to the consumer.

The third way is to build an alternative food system. Producers and consumers can choose to "opt out" of the current system and build their own. And people are doing it. Merely out of convenience, the stories in this book, of individuals circumventing the industrial food chain, are centered in the Midwest and Great Plains. But it's happening everywhere, and the pace of change is accelerating.

# Introduction

The individuals making a difference through their own backyard urban existence are genuinely passionate about producing and eating sustainably. Despite the pleasure produced by the act, no one talked to for this book ever used the word "hobby" to describe his or her activities. In interviews, the urban polyculture being practiced, whether in the backyard or on the restaurant rooftop, was always referred to as "farming," and the physical place was always a "farm." In fact, there is a trend towards giving these individually owned and operated backyard farmsteads names: "Freak Farm," "Zoo on Dawson," and my personal favorite, Maureen Cahill's "Moah's Ark." For the individuals, it is not an occupation, but neither is it frivolous; there are no "days off" when you have six milking goats and a dozen laying hens.

Other individuals have taken the passion a step further, and answered the call to entrepreneurship. Unlike the cultural and civil rights revolutions of the 1960's, it isn't America's youth leading the march to create sustainable food businesses. The people leading are, in my experience, people well into the middle innings of this game called life. I found this surprising at first; this kind of "change" seems harder to do once you have acquired dependents, or developed an income source that represents what economists call "an opportunity cost" when left behind for a new start. But by the end of the research for this book it made sense. Eckhart Tolle describes the inner peace that comes with pushing through the transition to live one's values:

> "There may be a period of insecurity and uncertainty. What should I do? As the ego is no longer running your life, the psychological need for external security, which is illusory anyway, lessens. You are able to live with

uncertainty, even enjoy it. When you become comfortable with uncertainty, infinite possibilities open up in your life. It means fear is no longer a dominant factor in what you do and no longer prevents you from taking action to initiate change."[1]

Tolle goes on to quote the Roman philosopher Tacitus, who observed, "the desire for safety stands against every great and noble enterprise."

This mid-life leap is not a trend without precedent. Gene Logsdon was about forty when he left his job in the big city and returned to his native Ohio to homestead and begin a prolific career as a writer. *You Can Go Home Again* tells that story and, I suspect, has in ways both big and small, inspired every reader who has turned its pages. Will Allen was in his forties when he could no longer ignore the internal compromises that provided for his comfortable, corporate existence. After a brief period of keeping one foot in both worlds, he committed to the creation of his non-profit, Growing Power, and later received a MacArthur Foundation "Genius Grant" for his efforts. Dan O'Brien kept cattle on his ranch for twenty years before raising the stakes at mid-life and switching to a small herd of bison.

In addition to the businesses, services, and regulatory trends highlighted in this book, the sustainable food trend might also benefit from a new school of economics. My own journey started when I made the connection between agriculture and both human and environmental health. By the end of the journey, it became clear that the web connecting food with human and environmental health was also inextricably linked to economic health. All that we use and benefit from, writes John Ikerd, is ultimately derived from nature. Measures of prosperity such as "gross domestic product," or GDP, don't seem as useful as they once did. If you total your car and wind up in the hospital, GDP goes up. Extract and sell all the natural resources below the surface, from potash to water to soil fertility, and GDP goes up, despite the fact that the nation is inherently less wealthy. This seems to be the kind of "madness" alluded to in the quote from Eckhart Tolle that opens this book. To paraphrase John Ikerd, the societies that failed in Jared Diamond's *Collapse* didn't acknowledge, like many economists, the finite limits nature places on society. "The economy is contained wholly and completely within the bounds of society and nature. The economy has no other sources of energy to create anything of economic value."[2]

Economics has even more that it can learn from nature. Just as biodiversity is critical to the sustainability of an ecosystem, and genetic diversity is critical to the survival of any species, so is diversity in producers, processors, and distributors to an economy. Diversity in crops and livestock is the secret to a farm staying ahead of the pests without the need for an abundance of chemical intervention. This issue of diversity in economics gets lost in the debate over whether a particular market is "free" or "regulated" as if one or the other is the goal to strive for. At the risk of getting bogged down in semantics, the target for policy should be neither a freer market nor a more regulated market; the target, in the case of the food business, should be a more *competitive* market. The specific attribute of competitive markets that sustainable food entrepreneurs are clamoring for, regardless of personal political philosophy, is *ease of entry* into the marketplace. Having so few companies control the processing and distribution of meat and dairy, for example, creates barriers to entry for alternative providers. As a result of industry consolidation, there are too few small-scale abattoirs available to aspiring livestock farmers.

Another way the current system creates a barrier to entry is the "one size fits all" body of regulations that govern the food industry. Regulations need to be scaled appropriately to allow new entrants to grow organically from a home-based business to a larger commercial operation down the road. The exemption for small quantities of on-farm poultry processing is an excellent example. You can start a computer business in your garage, why not a cheese business in your kitchen? We must consider trading, in the words of E. F. Schumacher, the idolatry of "giantism" for the virtues of smallness.[3]

If there is an arc to this narrative, it is wafer-thin and visible only to the author. With that said, the goal was to begin the discussion very narrow (small) and expand in scope before ending with big picture issues. The first section contains a brief history of the sustainable food movement generally, and the backyard chicken movement specifically. The phenomenon of chicken coops popping up in backyards all over America provides teachable moments that make the rest of the story easier to understand. Subsequent essays attempt to provide a view from the consumer's perspective, including profiles of individuals taking steps to eat sustainably.

Moving further along the food chain, the book talks about entrepreneurship in the sustainable food movement: which types of businesses are forming and which particular businesses *need* to be formed in order to have a real, sustainable local food network.

The later essays address sustainable agriculture's bigger picture, including the areas of investment, economics, and business hurdles participants in the movement will inevitably have to clear. I hope there is something useful in here for everyone. Everyone might also find at least one thing disagreeable; this is the byproduct of honesty, and not an attempt to be controversial for the sake of it. There isn't any one person with whom I agree on every detail of the sustainable food story, and I doubt that makes me unique.

Lastly, this was intended to be a book of ideas, but it ended up being as much about people. This seems fitting in hindsight. There are those who have decided that a values-based existence is worth the extra effort. There is no motivator quite like true character. When all of those individual exertions are consolidated, it becomes a movement. In his essay *The Whole Horse*, Wendell Berry wrote: "What agrarian principles implicitly propose…is a revolt of local small producers and local consumers against the global industrialism of the corporations. Do I think that there is hope that such a revolt can survive and succeed, and that it can have influence upon our lives and the world? Yes, I do." I do too.

# PART I

## How Did We Get Here?

# CHAPTER I

# Beyond Organic

*"The real work of planet-saving will be small, humble, and humbling, and (insofar as it involves love) pleasing and rewarding. Its jobs will be too many to count, too many to report, too many to be publicly noticed or rewarded, too small to make anyone rich or famous."* – Wendell Berry

Call me Chicken Man. My customers do. After twenty years working in investment management and corporate finance, I founded a delivery service to help people in Chicago keep backyard chickens. With little to interest me on the shores of the old money economy, I set sail. I may be crazy (time will tell), but I'm not alone.

In *Home Grown*, Brian Halweil paraphrases Jack Kloppenburg, a professor at the University of Wisconsin: There needs to be "something between Sysco and CSAs"…That void "may hold the greatest money-making opportunity for communities."[4] This book is about that void. It is a void not just between Sysco and CSAs; it is a void between farmer's markets. It is about the void between non-profit and industrial organic. In that void are thousands of entrepreneurs and millions of individuals who are already leading the shift. I hope to be one of them. Charity will unfortunately have its place for a very long time; food deserts (areas of the country without access to healthy food) aren't going away fast enough. The overall food industry, however, is simply too large to be carried on the back of volunteerism.

My transition didn't happen over night, and the food industry has been in transition for decades. I started eating organic twelve years ago, and I'd always been an outdoor enthusiast. I never saw any connection between my eating habits and the health of the environment. I barely saw a connection between my eating habits and my *own* health. In 2005, I read Jared Diamond's *Collapse* and James Howard Kuntsler's *The Long Emergency*. Then I read everything in Kuntsler's bibliography. I came to believe through that reading that eating sustainably was the single best thing I could do for both the environment *and* my personal health. I went from being an outdoor enthusiast to being an environmental advocate. I went from occasionally buying organic carrots to buying a share of production in a local organic farm (through a system called community supported agriculture, or CSA).

The bigger transition happened when these new values spilled over from my personal life into my professional life. I founded Backyard Chicken Run. I suddenly saw more reward in making $10,000 loans than from investing in publicly traded stocks. I was diving into the headwaters of the small but rapidly growing field of sustainable food. Today it's a rivulet. In the not too distant future, "local" food production will swamp the organic food movement in relevance. Along the way, the good food movement is creating bonds that obliterate socio-economic lines. From all walks of life, proponents of sustainable agriculture are awakening to a better way of eating, living, and potentially, working. For the local food movement to become more than a fringe subsector of the food industry, it needs more people to understand that great food can be great business.

### The Movement

Before jumping into the business of building a local food network, it is helpful to understand what got us here. If there were such a thing as a sustainable food continuum to chart the history of sustainable agriculture in the United States, it would start 50 years ago with the publication of Rachel Carson's book *Silent Spring*. An eloquent warning about the dangers of pesticides, it led to a ban on DDT in the United States 10 years later. Credited with launching the modern environmental movement, the book also launched the organic food movement. The organic food movement has made its mark on environmental advocacy while giving consumers an alternative to the chemical agriculture of the post-war era. This chemical or industrial agriculture is often referred to as conventional agriculture. The word "conventional" in this context would imply something ordinary and traditional, but in the near 10,000-year history of domesticated crops, there is nothing conventional about how farming is done in the United States today. That opinion can be applied to the large-scale production of vegetables and livestock as well as grains. I therefore don't use the phrase conventional agriculture except to be ironical. It otherwise distorts reality.

The definition of the word organic is also the source of increasing controversy. The United States Department of Agriculture (USDA) now owns and controls the word organic at least as it pertains to organic certification. Now that big processed food companies have acquired the majority of the pioneers in the organic food products space, the standards for what qualifies as organic are up for grabs. Out of necessity, this leads to a differentiation between "Big O" organic and "little o" organic. There may be inputs and processes that the USDA now deems acceptable when granting the certified organic designation that you, the consumer, would reject as organic. There are also requirements under the USDA organic standards that you might not necessarily require of a farmer who had worked successfully to gain your trust.

One example is the use of antibiotics. As farmers became the largest buyers of antibiotics, and antibiotics became a large part of the diet of animals in confined animal feeding operations, consumers of industrial beef, poultry, and dairy grew concerned about antibiotic resistance in humans. In reaction to this concern, the federal organic standards now prohibit any use of antibiotics in livestock, even if the animals get sick. A small-scale dairy farmer might choose a different path. Give the cow with an infection a dose of antibiotics, but take it out of the milking rotation until the drugs have cleared its system. In a certified organic operation, that animal would likely be destroyed or sold for a lower purpose, raising the cost of certified organic dairy to the consumer. How in the world is a sustainable food consumer supposed to make an informed decision about what is worth paying for and what is not?

The simple answer you will hear repeatedly in the sustainable food discourse, as well as this book, is "know your farmer." The tension between the "Big O" certified organic standards and both organic farmers and consumers created tinder for the local food movement. The consolidation of organic food brands by big packaged food companies provided the match. The "local" food movement is the next stage in the sustainable food continuum, and it is exploding. The rapid growth of farmers markets and community-supported agriculture attests to the trend. Through these two channels, the consumer can meet the farmer in person, ask questions, and develop trust. The consumer may even take the opportunity to visit the farm and satisfy any remaining curiosity or doubt about truth in advertising.

What then is *sustainable* food? I subscribe to an increasingly popular view that sustainable food is mostly organic and as local as possible. I say "mostly organic" because of the grey areas between "Big O" and "small o" organic standards. I say "as local as possible" because I still like to enjoy an avocado once in a while, and I've never seen one grown in Illinois.

Not all organic should be considered sustainable. Although this may soon change, a current example is the practice of feeding organic *corn* to cattle and calling the result organic beef. Feeding a diet exclusively comprised of corn to a ruminant animal such as a cow is unsustainable for many reasons. Simply put, it makes both the cow and the consumer sick. Growing "conventional" corn in order to feed cows erodes topsoil and pollutes our waterways. Meat of poor nutritional quality contributes to chronic disease in humans. This dynamic has given rise to the third and potentially most exciting phase of the sustainable food continuum, the grass-fed movement. Because the USDA's organic standards allow herbivores to be fed grain (and omnivores to be fed exclusively grain), a market has developed for what I call "pastured proteins," or livestock raised largely in a field of grass or pasture. The pastured proteins category includes grass-fed beef, pastured pork, and pastured broilers (meat birds) and egg layers. It could be the most exciting phase because perhaps more than any other product, raising beef, chicken, pork, dairy, and eggs sustainably fundamentally changes the nutritional content of the product. In fact, the consumer, the animal, *and* the environment will all be ultimately healthier. It is also a tremendous market opportunity for entrepreneurs in overalls.

## The Market

Despite decades of double-digit growth and the entrance of giants like Wal-Mart, organic food still has just a low single digit share of the trillion-dollar market for food in the United States. The local food market is even smaller and certainly overlaps with the organic sector. Grass-fed beef is smaller still as a percentage of its market.

But that's changing. It's changing as education in the consumer market shifts from the "inputs" to the "outputs" of sustainable agriculture. These outputs affect human health, the environment, food safety, and animal rights, just to scratch the surface. It represents a shift from a cost-based view of sustainable food to a benefits-based view. This is about what the world can *get* from eating sustainably.

What we *have* been getting is sick. Any discussion about our consumption of food invariably leads to the much-maligned Western diet. This diet is by many different estimates responsible for the largest chunk of chronic disease in the U.S. and therefore the majority of our healthcare expenditures. To paraphrase Wendell Berry, we are fed by a food industry, which pays no attention to health, and treated by a health industry, which pays no attention to food. Sadly, it is not a relationship that has served the people well.

The Western diet is usually associated with the intake of high-fat animal proteins, sugar, and processed foods. What the Western diet should also be associated with is *how* those animal proteins are produced; we do it differently here in the United States than just about anywhere in the world. It is the great red herring of the industrial food industry that organic food is no different nutritionally than conventionally produced food. Eggs are an easy example. Comparing the egg from a battery-caged hen to the egg from a sustainably raised hen isn't just comparing apples and oranges; it's comparing apples and fruit rollups. They are fundamentally different products. The sustainably produced egg looks and tastes different. It also contains less cholesterol and saturated fat than those supermarket eggs, but more vitamins, beta-carotene, and omega-3 fatty acids.[5] Grass-fed beef tells a similar story when compared to corn-fed beef. A decline in the nutrient content of vegetables through the years may also be traced back to how they are produced.[6] I'm not qualified, however, to determine if any of these referenced studies passed scientific muster. So how do we as consumers - and possibly investors - find the open door through all the smoke?

## The Method

As an institutional investor, I never had 100% of a story available to me. In making an investment decision, I was required to create a mosaic out of three different sources of material: facts, logic, and if available, personal experience. Armed with these tools, it was my challenge to come to an educated and sound conclusion. Consumers have to do the same thing when they go to the grocery store. Since the consumer must leave the store with something, he or she is "forced" to choose one product over another. The facts available to the consumer generally come from interested parties: food company marketing campaigns, the national organic standards board, and small studies done by Mother Earth News or the organic farmers themselves. In this battle for market share, the "facts" are fluid and no constituency is above reproach.

So, we move on to logic.

Your grandmother probably told you, "You are what you eat." I doubt there is anyone left who doesn't believe that to be true. If it's true for you, why isn't it true for an animal? If it's true that if you sit around eating

Twinkies all day you will end up looking like, well, a Twinkie, why isn't it true for a cow, chicken, or pig? It seems logical to me that if you feed an animal (or plant) a cruddy, unnatural diet, it will produce a cruddy, unnatural product in return. You are what you eat. An animal is what it eats. Therefore, you are what the animal eats (unless you are a vegan). How do you know what the animal is eating? Know your farmer.

Then, of course, there are personal experiences. Shame on the investor who buys the stock of a restaurant company without first experiencing a few of its meals. My own personal experience starts with a horrific lipid test result at the age of 42. According to my doctor, my total cholesterol was too high (to the extent that number is considered relevant anymore), the mix of good cholesterol to bad cholesterol was horrible (definitely not a *good* thing), and my triglycerides were off the charts (a bad result in any book). I was told to either give up meat and eggs or prepare to go on a statin (cholesterol lowering drug), presumably for the rest of my life. A passionate consumer of eggs in every form, and concerned about the long-term effects of maintenance drugs, I chose a third option. I started buying organic eggs from hens pastured on a farm in a neighboring county. In less than six months, my cholesterol had declined significantly and the other components of the lipid test moved to within the normal range. A year after getting my own backyard chickens, my total cholesterol also declined to normal, despite eating over a dozen eggs a week.

This raises an important point. Some people think that eating sustainably means living the life of an ascetic. I couldn't disagree more. Asking someone whether they eat to live or live to eat is a false dilemma. I am not sacrificing anything. I am eating all of the eggs, meat, and cheese my body craves, and eating *better tasting* eggs, meat, and cheese. Moreover, I am eating more local and organic vegetables as well, because they taste better with little (if any) preparation. At the same time, eating this way keeps agricultural chemicals out of my body and out of the environment. Does that matter? It does to me, and it should to you.

**The Story**

It is difficult to discuss human health and the environment separately, as important as they are to the story of sustainability. Personal and ecological health become inextricably linked the more deeply one digs in to them. Moreover, any discussion of economics must include a discussion about healthcare, which is such an increasingly large part of our economy. It is difficult to talk about *any* of these issues separately. John Muir's ecological aphorism about the web of life applies here too: pull on one thing, and you find it attached to everything else.

The story of agriculture and the environment begins with the Dead Zone in the Gulf of Mexico and works its way backwards. There are over 80 million acres dedicated to growing corn in the United States. Forty percent of the corn crop today goes to produce ethanol, and the majority of the rest goes to feed livestock (small minorities are either consumed by humans or exported). A nitrogen hog in agricultural parlance, corn requires staggering amounts of chemical fertilizer so it can be grown repeatedly on the same acreage. Excess amounts of nitrogen and phosphorous wash off the cornfields of the Midwest into creeks and streams that eventually feed the Mississippi River. The result is at first a *eutrophic*, or excessively nutrient-rich, environment. This causes algae blooms in waterways throughout the Mississippi River Basin and the Gulf of Mexico. The algae die after growing beyond the capacity of the host water to sustain it. This cradle to grave lifecycle of algae on steroids sucks the dissolved oxygen out of the water. Marine life in the now *hypoxic* (devoid of adequate oxygen) body of water either leaves the area or dies. Seafood-related businesses thus die in concert. Is this an environmental issue or an economic issue? It is both, of course.

The history of pesticide use in the post-war era resembles a game of *Whack-a-Mole*, erasing one problem with a solution that creates a new one somewhere else. Today's most popular and disconcerting pesticides weren't even around in Rachel Carson's time. The herbicide Atrazine was banned in Europe (where it is manufactured, ironically) due to ground water contamination and health risks. Atrazine remains widely used in the United States. Glyphosate (Round Up) is the most widely used herbicide in the United States. Weeds are becoming resistant to these herbicides. There was a 15-fold increase in the agricultural use of Round up from 1994 to 2005. Chemical use in agriculture is commensurate to anabolic steroid use in humans. After a big initial bang for the buck, returns diminish on increasing quantities of fertilizer and pesticides.[7]

Insecticides and herbicides represent not only an environmental hazard, but also a health hazard to the people employed to apply the chemicals. This unconventional method of farming doesn't protect us from illness; it breeds disease. If the purpose of agriculture is to make us sick, the American system is second to none. If the purpose of agriculture is to nourish, we have a long way to go.

Maybe this is the problem. As a society, we have diminished food production. We have lost sight of what agriculture can be. At its best, it can nourish the body and the spirit, and at its worst, it can bring a civilization to the brink. As in the case of Gandhi's reflection on the treatment of animals, our dominant methods of farming speak volumes about our culture. How food production, distribution, and consumption are organized is a reflection of our values. Wendell Berry said that eating is an agricultural act. Because of the broad reach that it has on so many segments of our existence, agriculture is also a moral act. When you, the consumer, choose one product over another, you set in motion a chain of events that can be traced back to a piece of land, to a farm hand, and to a philosophy of land use. You set in motion a chain of events that impacts someone thousands of miles away, and someone just downstream. More folks are saying enough is enough. But I'm not proselytizing; I'm just reporting what I see. Like wild animals heading to higher ground ahead of a tsunami, people are increasingly choosing not to participate in a system of agriculture (nor a way of doing business) that is starting to collapse under the weight of its own absurdity. We can either continue using the earth like a single-use disposable product, or choose instead a path of stewardship that acknowledges the interconnectedness of all things. We reap what we sow.

## The Beef

Beef consumption has taken a beating from a few different camps over the last four decades, and not just from practitioners in the fields of medicine and diet. Veganism and vegetarianism are admirable pursuits. In addition to health-related issues, individuals seem to make one of these lifestyle choices because of some combination of environmental and animal rights concerns. Sustainable farming addresses the environmental issues head on. Grass is a perennial; it doesn't generate the negative consequences of tilling, fertilizer, herbicides, and pesticides. Through manure management by Mother Nature, the grass services the needs of the animal, and the animal in turn services the needs of the grass.

Pasturing animals and feeding them a species-appropriate diet gives the animal a higher quality of life no matter the duration. In the end, literally, there is no getting around the issue of slaughter. Is it right for us to eat meat at all? Lacking a scientific background, I first appeal to the guiding hand of logic. I look in the mirror and open my mouth. Besides seeing evidence of neglect, I see molars for grinding, incisors for cutting, and canines for tearing. It looks to me like the mouth of an omnivore. There is no shortage of science to weigh in the balance, especially in the field of evolutionary biology. Relative to chimpanzees, the increase in brain size in what eventually became *Homo sapiens* apparently coincided with an increase in the consumption of meat. (A derivative theory, that instead of the meat's nutritional content, the complexity of *producing* a meal from meat might be what led to larger brain development, seems to me to put the sickle before the hoe.) The importance of animal fat in relation to human baby brain development lends credence to the idea that, especially in the developmental years, the human species is a machine that runs best on a well-rounded diet.

I have read that meat comprises 30% of the average American diet, but just 3% of that of a chimpanzee's. I also know that there are societies around the world that depend almost exclusively on animal protein, and experience much less chronic disease than Americans. I don't know if there is such a thing as the "right" percentage. I *do* know it takes twice as long to fatten cattle for market on pasture than it does when stuffing them with corn. Maybe the reduction in supply that would result from a wholesale switch to grass-fed beef would steer us in the right direction. Living at nature's pace, as author and homesteader Gene Logsdon would say. Wherever the cow chips fall, my contention is that it takes a smaller grass-fed steak to satiate the stomach compared to its corn-fed rival (as it should be with any nutritionally superior alternative). Less may actually be more.

### The Bottom Line

Despite some of the preceding melodrama, I am optimistic that change is coming for the better. Not because I am optimistic by nature or because I am visionary. I am optimistic that positive developments are afoot because it *has* to happen and I *see* it happening. The world of non-profits can't do it alone, however. Neither can government be expected to play the role of savior, except as it relates to scaling regulations appropriately for smaller businesses in the food production sector (including farms). *We the people* need to get off the sidelines and in to the game. As I said once already (and will say again), this shift is a fantastic business opportunity for local food entrepreneurs.

Farmers can't do it alone. Chefs have significant power to influence consumer behavior. Distribution challenges will have to be addressed by logistics and transportation professionals. Agronomists can find new ways for agriculture to work in harmony with nature instead of against it. Commercial kitchens are needed to foster specialty food entrepreneurs. Livestock processing should be done by the thousands of small operators that existed before the massive market share consolidation of the last sixty years. More regional organic feed producers are needed to supply the farmers and ranchers. Individual consumers will need to hack their way through a tangle of misleading advertising. Positive change will not come quickly or without great effort, but it will come.

This isn't a homesteading How-to guide. There are no suggested recipes, or specific lessons in eating seasonally. This is a book about the who, what, and why of the next phase of the sustainable food movement. With all due respect to Wendell Berry, this is an attempt to report at least *some* of those stories. Education and understanding are the seeds of motivation. Preaching to the converted is easy. Motivating the masses will be the real work of saving the planet.

# CHAPTER 2

## Pets with Benefits

"Help! My girls are out of food. They are running around the backyard eating some bugs and grass, but they are going to be starving pretty soon. Sorry for the short notice, but can you help me out?" – Rachel

Your first instinct, if you'd been the recipient of this email, would be to call child services or the police. I did neither. I loaded up my van with feed, grit, crushed oyster shells, and chicken scratch, and into the city of Chicago I went, making seven different stops, of which Rachel was the first. Rachel and her family keep hens (her "girls") for pets, four of them to be exact, in a backyard chicken coop. Hens are often referred to as "pets with benefits" in backyard chicken circles. "Pets" because they are gentle, calming, and interesting creatures that will bond with any owner brave enough to raise them from chicks. The benefits come in the form of delicious eggs, or as Three Stooges fans refer to them, hen fruit. Yes, people keep hens in the city, and in cold places like Chicago. It is impossible to know how many, but I am comfortable saying that there are hundreds of families doing it in the city of Chicago and hundreds more in its suburbs. There are over 2,500 backyard coops in Portland. Backyard chickens are also popular in Atlanta. A blog on BackyardChickens.com has over 170,000 followers. People are doing it in the north and in the south. They are doing it in the suburbs and in the city. It is being done on tiny urban lots and on rooftops.

The reasons people are embracing chickens in their backyards are the same reasons people find the sustainable food movement to be attractive overall. Moreover, like the sustainable food movement generally, participants in the backyard chicken movement come from all walks of life. The rise of backyard chickens across America provides a decent framework for understanding the secular trend towards eating and living sustainably. Folks who make the effort to eat sustainably do so because of concerns over the environment, personal health, animal rights, and energy use. Data on the rate of growth in backyard chicken coops isn't available on a national level and much of the movement remains underground. More than a casual observer, I would wager that the double-digit growth rate in farmers markets in the United States would prove modest when compared to the growth in backyard coops.

As far as eating food that is made "locally," it doesn't get any more local than your backyard. Just like having a vegetable garden, there is no getting in your car to go to the store to buy something that on average, according to the Aldo Leopold Center for Sustainable Agriculture, comes from 1,500 miles away. But there is so much more to this "locally made" phenomenon than just saving on gas. Americans have learned a lot lately about how their food is produced, and they don't like what they've learned; livestock are fed a diet designed to fatten the animal at the lowest cost. This diet includes large quantities of antibiotics, not as a short-term treatment for infection, but as food for growth enhancement. Over exposure to antibiotics in humans, animal rights, genetically modified organisms. The list of the reasons consumers are taking the matter of producing some of that food into their own hands goes on and on and is covered elsewhere. They are turning away from a system that breeds suspicion along with disease. Since trust in food producers moves inversely with distance from the source, these *locavores* shop labels based not only on ingredients and country of origin, but also on city and state of origin.

But with backyard chickens, consumers don't even have to go shopping. So back to the eggs.

Eggs are the gateway drug of the sustainable food movement. I can't think of any food item that when produced in the backyard is so superior to its store-bought alternative (though the tomato comes close). It is superior in quality, taste, appearance, and nutritional content. But "produced" may be the wrong word. In the case of my own hens, I don't *produce* anything. I feel more like a shepherd. I protect them from harm and give them access to what they need to be happy and healthy. Nature takes care of the rest.

And what a job nature does. A single large egg weighs less than 2 ounces, yet the USDA considers the egg to be "one of nature's most complete foods." [8] It has the highest form of protein available. As already mentioned, the sustainably produced egg has lower cholesterol and saturated fat compared to the conventionally produced eggs you find at the supermarket. Relative to its size, a single egg provides a disproportionate percentage of the recommended daily dose of vitamins and minerals.

Aside from the nutritional content of the egg, it is the egg's shell that is most amazing, because it provides a natural protection against contamination. Although the shell is permeable (according to one source, the chicken's eggshell actually has 9,000 pores that allow air and moisture to pass through), this permeability does not lead to a risk of infection. Mother Nature made sure of that. A freshly laid egg has a sort of film that coats the shell called a bloom or cuticle. The bloom reduces moisture loss and prevents bacteria from entering the egg. While the USDA recommends immediate refrigeration to 40 degrees Fahrenheit in order to prevent the growth of salmonella (which could be passed from the mother hen if she was already infected), there is, in fact, no rush to refrigerate an egg from a healthy hen while the bloom is on the shell. If you have the good fortune to visit a small grocery store in southern Europe, you might still see egg cartons stacked on the end cap of an aisle instead of a refrigerator.

Once you experience the thrill of a few chickens producing natural miracles in your own back yard every day, you're hooked. You know sustainable living means better, tastier, more easily accessible food. You know the food is safe and nutritious because you know *exactly* how it came to be. And you want more of it. So you might try a backyard beehive or take your first taste of raw milk. Maybe you start making your own cheese. After trying just a few eggs, your perception of eating is altered; embracing local food is a rush, not a chore.

## A Little About Chickens

Maybe the chicken's story should have come before the egg's. Depending on breed, a hen will start laying eggs around 5 or 6 months of age. Believe it or not, you don't need a rooster to get a hen to lay eggs. Instead of monthly ovulation, as in the case of the human female, a hen will ovulate daily under perfect conditions. What a hen (also called a "layer" at this stage, for obvious reasons) is actually doing is dropping an unfertilized egg. If you ever wanted to hatch chicks from a hen's eggs, then yes, a rooster is required. The hen will lay eggs for roughly one year, and then go through a mid-life crisis of sorts, called a "molt." Perhaps the awkwardness of puberty is a better analogy. Either way, the hen will lose lots of old feathers and egg laying will be temporarily disrupted. Eventually, the hen will grow new feathers and resume a regular laying schedule, but this time with larger eggs compared to the first year. She will continue to lay for another year or so, and then the "productive" period of her life (as far as regular egg laying is concerned) will come to an end.

Chicken eggs come in all different colors and sizes depending on the breed. Different breeds of hens might lay eggs with white, brown, tan, green, blue, or even speckled shells. Brown shells (or any color for that matter) do not imply that eggs are organic. A "bantam" or smaller version of a standard breed lays smaller eggs. These variables, as well as the appearance, personality, and hardiness of the bird, should be taken into consideration when an owner picks a breed of chicken.

Hardiness is a consideration of some consequence if you live in a cold climate such as Chicago's. Though this claim is often met with disbelief, if you have a properly structured chicken coop and a sufficient number of hens, you do not need supplemental heat in your chicken coop. I say sufficient number of hens because the girls will roost wing to wing and keep each other warm on cold nights. My favorite cold weather breeds are the Rhode Island Red and Barred Plymouth Rock. Because I wouldn't want to keep less than three hens and premature death of a pet chicken is not uncommon (because the bird either succumbs to sickness or a predator), I consider it prudent to start with a minimum of four chickens. Although the coop should offer your hens protection from cold winds, it is also important to have a vent at the coop's peak. In the summer time, this vent serves the purpose of releasing any ammonia generated by composting litter in the coop, and in the winter, the vent releases moisture that otherwise might collect on the chicken's comb and thus cause frostbite.

The environmental benefits of backyard chickens touch upon nearly every negative aspect of our current industrial food system. First and foremost is the reduction in "food miles" to zero. Allowing your hens to graze in the grass will reduce the amount of poultry feed you need to buy, and there is no egg carton to dispose of or recycle. The shell itself can be crushed and tossed into your compost pile (or directly under a tomato plant, which will treasure the calcium). The paper bag containing your chicken feed can be sent to recycling. Even the chicken manure, considered "black gold" by organic farmers because of its high nitrogen content, can be accumulated in the straw on the floor of the chicken coop and composted on site. I use my chicken coop as a composter for all vegetable-based food waste: toss those turnip greens and waste from the juicer directly into the coop, and what the chickens don't eat they will churn into the litter. I also use what is known as the "deep litter" method of litter management. I periodically layer on fresh pine shavings or straw as the year goes on, allowing real-time composting in the coop with the help of hens that continually scratch and turn the bedding. I may only empty and change the litter in the coop completely a few times a year.

If you are lucky enough to be able to let your hens free range in the yard, you will notice a distinct benefit in the egg's appearance, indicating an additional benefit in nutritional content. The yolk will be closer to bright orange than yellow, a result of the beta-carotene in the grass the hens consume. This coloring can put some consumers on their heels at first. To paraphrase Gene Logsdon again, few of them have ever seen a "healthy" egg.

The improvement in animal rights is obvious. Instead of being kept in a battery cage, unable to turn around and surrounded by an incomprehensible number of other hens in the same circumstance, your backyard hen lives the life a chicken was truly meant to live – running around like Rachel's girls, eating grass and bugs. Her contentedness directly impacts the quality of the eggs. Stress changes hormone levels and alters physiology in animals just as it does humans, so it seems to me that a stress-free hen will produce eggs that are better for me.

### Changing the Rules

Once you are informed about the behavior of a healthy, free-ranging hen, it will be difficult for you to support battery cage economics (and it *is* all about economics). I am not arguing that a hen is as smart as a dog, but neither is it a fish swimming in circles all day unaware that it is repetitiously covering the same waters. My hens can actually recognize the bag of freeze-dried mealworms I stock and bring out occasionally. Mealworms are their favorite treat. (Somewhere a commercial poultry farmer just choked reading that sentence; mealworms are very expensive.) No matter where I am in the backyard, if my hens see me with that little green plastic bag in my hand, they come flying (in chicken fashion, twelve inches off the ground with the occasional touch down) toward me as fast as their wings and legs can manage. If they don't see me, I need only shake the bag, and the sound alone generates a Pavlovian response.

People keep parakeets, snakes, tarantulas, turtles, and rodents as pets. The major difference between these animals (or cats and dogs, for that matter) and a chicken is that the chicken also provides a utility other than companionship: eggs. In my opinion, that utility has desensitized humans to their treatment. Opponents of the backyard chicken movement will quickly argue that "pets" come into the house at night and chickens are merely "livestock." There is only one definition of livestock in my Webster's New World College Dictionary (Third Edition): "domestic animals kept for use on a farm *and raised for sale and profit*" (emphasis added). Chickens are domesticated, but I'm not keeping them for sale or profit. So what are they? The reality is that backyard chickens fail to fit neatly into any modern categorization of pets or livestock, because they provide the benefits of both. This concept of needing new rules for a new millennium is going to be a recurring theme in the story of the local food movement, especially as it relates to regulation. All the suburban homesteading knowledge in the world doesn't help you if you can't legally do what you want to do. Consequently, I get as many questions about how to change a village's backyard chicken laws as I get about how to keep backyard chickens. So please forgive what seems like a random diversion in the section that follows.

## Changing the Code

As of this writing in early 2012, backyard chickens are legal in 95 of the top 100 cities in America. But legal hens are more the exception than the rule in the suburbs, despite the larger building lots. Be aware that your legal challenges may not begin or end with your village. If you are unfortunate enough (as I have been) to be subjected to a Home Owners Association (HOA) and its Board, it may not matter what (if anything) you succeed in getting changed down at town hall. It is unlikely that a typical HOA will have rules that are more lenient than those in the larger village, but it can certainly have more restrictive rules. Undeterred by the lack of restriction against keeping backyard chickens in my neighborhood's HOA code, the Board decided to prosecute me for a violation of *village* code. To the Board's great surprise, I went to the village to get the code amended.

How to get a town's backyard chicken regulations changed is a topic of great discussion among aspiring hen owners. I can't tell you that there is a silver bullet to getting your local code changed. I was successful in getting the code changed, but it took twelve months, and the new code is the most expensive and burdensome affirmative code in existence. I don't go around bragging about it. Still, there is learning to be shared.

When someone asks me, "What is the best way to fight your town to get the backyard chicken restrictions lifted?", my first advice is this; don't fight them. Work with them. Stay with a message that conveys what an incredibly positive development sustainable living can be. In a country where we share the burden of pollution as well as the cost of healthcare, if your neighbors want to live sustainably, let them. Encourage them. It is in your self-interest, even if you yourself want to eat corn-fed beef and battery cage eggs. It might ultimately result in a cleaner world and lower taxes for you.

Next, quickly diffuse panic by reminding the council members that your village would not be carving new territory out of the wilderness by making backyard chickens legal. As previously stated, it is being done all over the country. The city of Orlando, Florida, recently approved the issuance of permits as part of a limited one-year test program. New cities are joining the list every month. This point is especially relevant when it comes to the next most important maneuver: debunking the fear mongering that is inevitably going to rise out of the "against" camp like ammonia off a pile of manure.

There are many negative myths about keeping backyard chickens, but the first three are usually already covered by any town or city code under a "general nuisance" clause. General nuisances are things such as noise, mess, and smell. I always like to argue that since a township with a general nuisance ordinance already has the power to prosecute a citizen for being too loud, messy, or malodorous, there is no need for a whole new code governing backyard chickens. Just make them legal. That argument has not yet worked. Prepare to become fluent in chicken behavioral science as a consequence.

Roosters are loud, and they don't lay eggs. Therefore, backyard chicken keepers rarely own roosters. Roosters will most likely be banned by any affirmative code (though they are legal in the city of Chicago), and you should let that one go. Hens are not loud compared to either dogs or humans. Measured in decibels, your normal conversational voice is similar to a hen merely expressing her hen-ness. Moreover, a hen spends most of her time scratching, eating, and taking dust baths (i.e., frolicking in the dirt). Contrary to popular belief, hens don't "bawk" all day. Hens might simply become more boisterous right after laying an egg. It's a victory song, like a "Hail to the Victors" for chickens, without the marching band. If you consider the energy it takes for a four-pound hen to lay 250 eggs a year, you will agree that she's earned the right to crow a little. My hens sing this victory song for about a minute and a half after laying. Meanwhile, a dog is often allowed to bark incessantly from sun up to sun down without any repercussions. I like to argue that backyard chickens should be governed no differently than dogs and cats. That one hasn't worked yet either.

"Mess and smell" are often both associated with chicken manure, but there are some reasons to analyze them separately. Manure is the most obvious way for a chicken to make a mess, but if spread around the yard by a free-range chicken, and assuming your flock isn't out of proportion with the size of your lot, it should scarcely be noticeable. A hen is small, and so is its poop.

Chicken manure that is concentrated in one smaller area such as a coop can be a different, smelly story, but it does not have to be. In addition to being a shelter from the storm, it is helpful to think about your chicken coop as a compost bin or the litter on the floor of the coop as a compost pile. A proper compost pile has a certain "carbon to nitrogen" ratio that allows the organic material to biodegrade efficiently and without smell. If your compost pile smells, your "C-N" ratio is out of whack. Since chicken manure is very high in nitrogen, a smelly coop most likely means that it is lacking substantial carbon relative to manure in the mix. The "carbons" are also called the "browns" in composting parlance: straw, pine shavings, mulch, etc. Pine shavings are generally much higher in carbon content than straw. Therefore, sprinkling a few fistfuls of pine shavings over a manure-covered base of straw (typical bedding material) can quickly stem the odor. It isn't that the smell of pine is necessarily going to mask the smell of manure; the pine shavings are literally getting the carbon-nitrogen ratio back to where it needs to be.

Another source of mess in the minds of concerned citizens and bureaucrats is the chicken feed itself. I like to argue that if you are going to outlaw backyard chickens due to a fear over messy poultry feed, you also need to outlaw messy bird feeders. (A chicken is a bird, after all). Add this argument to the list of exercises in logic that will not win the day. Regulations permitting backyard chickens will likely require that feed be kept in a secure container, or even in the house, lest it attract vermin.

You are also likely to hear that backyard chickens will attract rats. This is naturally more of a concern in urban areas than in the suburbs. Whenever I hear this argument in Chicago, I picture two rats up in Waukegan (a town on Lake Michigan north of the city) drinking coffee and reading the newspaper:

"Hey, Norton, check this out."

"What's up, Ralphie?"

"They got backyard chickens down in Chicago. If we hurry, we can catch the 3 o'clock train and be there for dinner."

"Let's go!"

If you have rats in your city, they were there long before you got there, and they'll be there long after you are gone, chickens or no chickens. If the rats are attracted to chicken coops, they'll be coming to my backyard, not yours. If rats are coming to my backyard because of my chickens, odds are I'm not going to be keeping chickens much longer (being as repulsed by the thought of rats as anybody). Non-problem solved.

In the suburbs, the "pest concern" is actually coyotes rather than rats. With just a little bit of research you will discover that among a coyote's favorite meals are goslings. If we are going to ban backyard chickens because of a fear of coyotes, then we should ban geese from our town. As with the rats, if coyotes are coming to my backyard, they will hopefully figure out they can't get in to the coop and move on. Energy expended on hunting is a precious commodity to a wild animal; it will not be frivolously wasted. The usual legislative response is to require predator-proof housing for your birds. If the chickens are your pets, you should want to do this anyway.

I refer to a final "catch all" category of fictional fears as "bird dogs and bullshit." In responding to claims in this category, one should gather current data points quantifying how widespread backyard chicken activity is in the United States. (As I said, the data changes every month.) If the opposition says they are concerned that property values are going to go down, demand to see the data. (There is no data supporting that claim.) Your research is more likely to show a secular trend toward "green communities" suggesting a very different outcome. Before one particular speaking engagement, I had a curmudgeonly audience member betray his true feelings with a faux expression of middle-of-the-road pragmatism. "Well, I can see how someone who spends a million dollars on a home *might* not want to have to look out on his neighbor's chickens." Yes, I said, and I can imagine how someone spending a million dollars on a home might want to be left alone in his own backyard. I deliver chicken feed to some of the most exclusive communities on Chicago's North Shore. Don't tell me about property values.

If the opposition expresses a concern over some disease you have never heard of, again respond by asking to see the data. There is enough history and experience out there that if it were going to happen, it would have happened somewhere. A council member in a town in Illinois expressed concern over *histoplasmosis* (a flu-like infection contracted from inhaling fungus spores found in soil containing bird and bat droppings) floating over the fence and infecting neighbors. Banning backyard chickens because of a fear of *histoplasmosis* is as logical as confiscating my barbeque grill because the smoke is going to choke a neighbor to death. Still, go ahead and show me the data.

When it comes to potential diseases, you should anticipate answering questions about avian flu, or "bird flu," specifically the highly pathogenic H5N1 virus (because of its unique ability to jump from birds to humans). I am not aware of a single documented case of H5N1 in the

Western Hemisphere involving chickens. According to the Center for Disease Control, dogs killed over 300 people in the United States between 1979 and 1996.[9] Yet, we haven't banned dogs.

Some arguments against keeping backyard chickens are so irrational that it becomes difficult to formulate a response. I witnessed one councilwoman state in a public hearing that she was worried about getting sued in the event her "bird dogs" (Labrador retrievers one presumes) got so excited at seeing a neighbor's chickens the dogs might run through the electric fence and kill a chicken. I still don't know what to do about that one. Amnesty for bird dogs?

Though the process may continue for months, your bid to change your local code will likely succeed or fail during the very first public hearing. To further increase your chances of successfully amending your local code, try to win the debate *before* that first night. Sit down with an influential member of the town council and have an intelligent, unemotional discussion without the noise and pressure of a public hearing. You can succeed without it, but having a champion on the inside will greatly increase your chances of success.

**Opportunity Knocks**

Once backyard chickens become legal in your area, the movement offers several growing opportunities for aspiring entrepreneurs. Not all backyard chicken keepers feel comfortable building their own coops. Although professional carpenters have seized upon the opportunity, you don't need to be a brilliant craftsman to make some extra money building chicken coops. Chicago even has its own "chicken consultant" who will come to your home to review your setup and answer any questions you might have about the appearance and health of your birds. Chicken keepers will also need supplies not readily found at the corner (or "big box") pet store. That is an opportunity for garden centers and pet stores. It is also what led to the creation of my company, Backyard Chicken Run.

# CHAPTER 3

......................................

## Backyard Chicken Run

"We wander between two worlds, one dead, one power-less to be born" – Matthew Arnold

I'm dropping the order on the customer's back porch as I do more times than not. I turn to head back to the van when I see a scantily clad woman behind the screen door. She meets me halfway across the deck and grabs a fistful of curly hair on the back of my head. She starts licking my ear: First the lobe, then the ticklish inner sanctum...

Wait. I'm bald. I've never had curly hair and what I have left is buzzed to a bristle. Suddenly her breath smells like wet dog hair. I open my eyes to see Cody the Wonder Mutt (and recently rescued shelter dog) standing over me. Only on an episode of *Sex and the City* do my brethren in brown uniforms get to share horizontal refreshments with the ladies while on duty. I bounce out of bed anyway, grateful for remaining faithful to my wife of 16 years, and grateful to Cody for keeping me from oversleeping. There are two seasons in Chicago: winter and construction season. For these and other reasons, the traffic can be more stifling than the humidity in July, especially if you don't get off the Kennedy Expressway by 7 am. That means I have to be on the road by 5.

I do not believe that I needed to be humbled, humbling though the days can be. Despite the physical challenge, it isn't the work that humbles me most. This delivery business is humbling because it puts me in the presence of such decent souls making efforts that in the whole production may seem mundane but individually are rather grand. No one could make a greater mistake, said Edmund Burke, than he who did nothing because he could do only a little. That spirit is on brilliant display in the sustainable food movement, where many individuals are seizing small opportunities to make their own and others' lives more sustainable and more rewarding.

Carl Jung described neurosis as the suffering of the soul which has not discovered its own meaning. Managing money for institutions and the wealthy was fun and challenging. It was also a spiritually bankrupt profession. Since founding Backyard Chicken Run, I have had customers hug me, write me thank you notes, and ask their Creator to throw me a bone. To spin Jung slightly, life has no meaning other than what you give to it. The process of discovery is life's great journey. This intangible reward is an important reason why consumers and entrepreneurs are flocking to the sustainable life – and in the process they are creating a sustainable economy.

It all started innocently enough. It was an altruistic effort to help a group of people I admired. Alone in the office for much of 2009, I had plenty of quiet time with which to contemplate the coming decade. When not analyzing individual companies, I digested years of reading on the environment, agriculture, and business. Through that process I became convinced that sustainability was going to be the best secular growth opportunity of the coming decade. In the spring I applied to a Masters program for Environmental Studies, and later in the year signed up for my first homesteading class, a three-hour course in keeping backyard chickens. It was offered through an Illinois CSA, Angelic Organics. Specifically, Martha Boyd of the Angelic Organics "Urban Initiative" organized the backyard chicken program. Here was a farm (Angelic Organics) two hours outside of Chicago, reaching out to city dwellers to teach them to be more self-sufficient when it came to their own food. Even as I think about it years later, I am in awe of the vision and the effort. The Urban Initiative also serves as a reminder of how non-profit outreach can seed the new, for-profit economy needed to move the food sector towards sustainability.

Having completed the three-hour class, I provided my contact information so that I could join an online discussion group called Chicago Chicken Enthusiasts. This board was another brilliant idea. Even if a student left with a question unanswered or a doubt in his or her heart, he or she could join this online bulletin board and pose questions to a group comprised of experienced backyard chicken keepers. More importantly, this was a group of Chicago-based backyard chicken keepers who felt passionately about mentoring aspiring "urban farmsteaders." Martha's job didn't stop with organizing semi-annual courses on raising chickens; she made sure that the Chicago Chicken Enthusiasts were advocates for *responsible* chicken keeping. She was nurturing a movement and didn't want it set back by irresponsible behavior. Martha kept a close eye on any initiatives that would restrict keeping backyard chickens. Not all the aldermen in the city of Chicago were supportive. Getting in front of negative news stories by making sure they never happened in the first place has been a big part of Martha's legacy.

I logged on to the Chicago Chicken Enthusiasts website that first night and started to read the posts. Every technical question regarding keeping backyard chickens was met with an answer from an experienced practitioner. Most of the questions, however, were not about *how* to perform the tasks associated with backyard coops. Most of the questions were about how and where does one *get* the stuff needed to sustain a backyard coop. You don't need a lot of equipment and supplies, but what you need is not available on every street corner. In addition to the chicken coop itself, a list of basic backyard chicken supplies includes feed, hanging waterers and feeders, crushed oyster shells, and grit. The most common request was for guidance about procuring *organic* chicken feed. There was one pet store on the south side of the city that carried chicken supplies, but management refused to carry organic feed. For someone living in Chicago in 2009, the only way to buy organic poultry feed was to drive out of Cook County to places like Michigan and northwestern Illinois (though some folks were having it shipped in from even further away). Many of those participating in the discussion did not own cars. Folks were carpooling to drive out to the country to get organic chicken feed. One woman was renting a vehicle from Zip Car for a couple hours. Think about that for a second. She was renting a car for $25 to drive two hours round trip for a $25 bag of organic chicken feed. That was *not* my idea of sustainability.

That was, however, my idea of commitment to an ideal. I have enormous respect for people that live their values. If I didn't yet have the guts to join this movement by getting my own chickens, at least I could participate by helping others live sustainably.

I started a new thread on the discussion board and offered to come through the city once a week with whatever supplies people needed. The economics of my proposition were simple; I would drop the order off at the customer's door and charge no more than folks were already paying. I didn't make any thoughtful calculations before memorializing the post by hitting the return button. The act was more of an impulse than a well-constructed plan. Regardless, I entered the post on the discussion board, shut down my computer, and started the ritual of feeding, bathing, and reading to my sons before putting them to bed.

I logged back on a couple hours later. I had seven customers and Backyard Chicken Run was born.

Customers emailed me their first orders in December 2009. I made my first deliveries in January. I was using my Toyota Highlander Hybrid, a readily available green choice for a delivery vehicle. I'd been hanging out at Broken Fence Farm near Woodstock, Illinois for several months trying to gain some experience in sustainable agriculture. Proprietor Susie Jeppsen let me piggyback on her organic feed orders. For everything else, I paid retail at a Farm and Fleet and just passed along the cost. I made deliveries on Sunday mornings, and each customer (usually) left me a check under the doormat.

Through word of mouth alone, I seemed to pick up a new customer every week. Moreover, one customer requested I bring the dog food she had historically picked up on her long-range feed runs. This development, and the fact that not every customer remembered to leave me a check, prompted the development of a website with ordering capability. Not wanting to spend much money on this endeavor, I chose to build a website with a shopping cart on my iMac instead of paying someone to do it. In less than four hours, I had loaded pictures of each item and added a button for purchase. By taking credit cards and having accurate delivery addresses with the order forms, Backyard Chicken Run went back to requiring minimal effort.

A year later, I added a second delivery day each week. My Highlander was proving inadequate for the demands of growing orders. I sold it and with the proceeds bought a cargo van for deliveries and a Prius for people moving. The pet supply delivery business is still small relative to the industry overall, but it's growing every month. It will continue to grow because more and more people will see the value in living sustainably. It will also grow because the challenges faced by the delivery model (traffic jams, rising gas prices, etc.) are the same things that make the service attractive. Providing delivery services will be a growth industry for a long time.

I started focusing on Backyard Chicken Run full time in the fall of 2011, a year after shutting down my investment management company. Like *Coop* author Michael Perry, I'm actually partial to labor. I thrive on work that keeps the body busy but frees the mind "to ponder." That pondering continues to lead me to new ventures related to the sustainable food movement. Each opportunity seems small, but none is unimportant.

# PART II

## The Sustainable Consumer

# CHAPTER 4

## City Life

"Beset by violence, economic instability, and ecological deterioration over which we seem to have no control, we feel helpless. The human race has become afraid of itself. In this quandary, people are trying to take their lives back into their own hands…individuals are taking steps to at least secure their homes – their food supply, their fuel supply, and their shelter. They are establishing homeland security not as political farce but in the vital, original meaning of the term." - Gene Logsdon, *All Flesh Is Grass*

Logsdon goes on to say in the introduction of *All Flesh Is Grass* that many are actually making their stand "right within the urban world." You're darn right they are. The opportunities to help city living green itself are a practically endless. And those opportunities reflect a continuum of "skill" level as broad as the general population is diverse. Even the courageous do-it-yourselfers profiled in this section need, at a minimum, supplies and sometimes very task-specific tools. As the "early adopter" phase of the green living movement gives way to a broader cross section of the population, those newcomers will most likely need more help, more services, more solutions-in-a-box, to get their backyard farmstead operational. In a nutshell, imagine all of the opportunity that exists in assisting the less adventurous among us to eat just as well as the pioneers I have had the pleasure of meeting through Backyard Chicken Run.

# Urbanization

The "back to the land" movement appears to have given way to the back to the city movement. Human populations around the globe continue to flock to cities, and I see it as a secular trend here in the United States. A mass movement to homesteading on acreage as a solution to our environmental problems isn't going to happen, and may have been misguided to begin with. Stewart Brand, in *Whole Earth Discipline: An Ecopragmatist Manifesto*, talks about the back to the city movement as part of a multipronged solution to climate change. The more people there are living vertically, the more opportunities there will be for nature to take back open spaces. City dwellers can live without cars and tend to have fewer children. Infrastructure efficiencies contribute significantly to the environmental superiority of cities over sprawl. Cities "are becoming the Greenest thing humanity does for the planet."[10] We have the ability to "green" rooftops, garden in the backyard, and raise chickens.

I share the following stories of sustainable living pioneers for multiple reasons. First, I think they serve as examples of what can be done. I hope they are inspirational. But because very few people will have the confidence (or skill) to do all the things these pioneers were able to do on their own, the business opportunity resides in helping the next wave of aspiring pioneers become more self sufficient. Developing expertise in just one of the facets of sustainability is an instant consulting opportunity. Then there are the materials required, which may not be readily available in the city, from building supplies, gardening supplies, and seeds. Entire industries exist to "help" the average person be more like famous athletes, successful business people, or beautiful models. As you read the stories of these thought and action leaders, imagine the opportunities in making the sustainable urban lifestyle more attainable to the general public.

## The Rooftop Farm

It was mild for a January day in Chicago when I toured a customer's rooftop farm. Cold was coming though; in 24 hours, the temperatures would drop to below zero for the first time in over a year. Wind chill would move us to negative double digits, a place where exposed skin starts to hurt after a few minutes. But this day was relatively pleasant, all things considered.

The "farm tour" may as well have started in the building's top floor apartment kitchen. Herbs hanging to dry, cabinets with glass doors offering a peak at homemade canned goods, and a freezer full of vegetables. Even if you didn't know there were a dozen raised beds on the roof over your head, you would believe that this kitchen was the expression of people who cared about food. The food itself could have come from anywhere, of course. It could have come from the building's first floor tenant and one of Chicago's premiere food co-ops, the Dill Pickle. Some of it likely did. But most of it came from the building's canopy.

Dave Vondle is the building's owner and resident craftsman. A designer by profession and an engineer by education, to a layperson such as myself, he is also an artist when it comes to creating things both beautiful and functional. The expert grower in the apartment is Breanne Heath, trained in soil science and employed by Growing Home, a nonprofit organization dedicated to making Chicago a greener city through organic agriculture.

The first level of the two-tiered roof holds the chicken coop, the most recent addition to the household's food production system and the reason I was there. From here you can also look over the edge to the alleyway where a system of rain barrels collects, moves, and pumps water up to the rooftop. Each raised bed is its own "zone" and is watered electronically from a panel on the wall in the kitchen below. Despite the application of such sophisticated mechanics and electronics, a folded ladder leaning up against the wall of the rooftop's second tier is the only way up to the vegetable farm.

I'd been on this roof once before at the height of the growing season. It was a feast for the eyes, and it would become a feast for the stomach: beet red stalks, orange and yellow fruit, and leaves every shade of green.

Vegetables, grapes, hops and kiwi came together in this Eden in the sky. Watermelon hung, each in its own personal hammock, from the archway at the north end of the roof. It was very different in January, obviously. On this day, the beds were mostly gray and brown, life returning to the soil in death and decay so new life can come forth in the spring. A couple of red chard plants, standouts in any garden for their radiance, remained vertical but seemed too proud, considering the harsh climate around the corner. In a small cold frame built atop a raised bed, a mature kale plant on the verge of flowering still stood defiantly, looking more like a miniature palm tree than kin to cabbage.

The original plan was rather modest: reinforce the rooftop to grow some grasses, maybe even bamboo. But it's unnatural for great minds to think small, and as the project grew, so did the expertise and the community involvement. Dave worked with a structural engineer to maximize both growing space and growing *depth*. Breanne wanted twelve inches of growing material, and that brings with it a lot of weight. The "bending moment" of the beams and shear load along the walls meant that these heavy beds should be pushed to the perimeter of the rooftop. If there was a disappointing moment in the process of building the rooftop farm, it was when it came time to source the materials that would protect the roof. LEED (Leadership in Energy and Environmental Design) consultants were all the rage at the time, yet none were willing to provide an answer to the simple question of what manufacturers Vondle could turn to for the drainage layer. Fortunately, contractors were more than willing to provide the information for free. The sustainable food movement, in my experience, has been characterized by an incredible amount of camaraderie and cooperation. Though not always so, most everyone I have come across is eager to share. (Along this line, Dave introduced me to a fascinating community working under the name "farmhack." Farmhack has been working to democratize information related to sustainable agriculture. To use a software industry analogy, it is an open source model for young farmers looking to succeed with sustainable practices.)

Even outside financial resources were publicly available to pay for the construction costs. If Dave hadn't been able to use TIF (tax increment financing) funds from his ward's alderman to build out both the Dill Pickle space and the roof, there was a Green Roof Grant available from the city of Chicago. It is interesting to pause and recognize the many different resources and types of organizations that played roles in this story. Dave contributed his own hard-won capital and expertise from a career as a designer. Breanne contributed expertise developed through her own education and work for a non-profit. There are the for-profit businesses: the consumer cooperative, the LEED consultants, and the vendors of building and gardening supplies. Moreover, local government structured two separate programs that, though not in such abundance that they could provide funding to all comers, helped early-movers get out of the starting gate and on the way to a more sustainable lifestyle. On this last point, it's worth noting how the city government (in this case, Chicago) is trying to create a supportive regulatory environment, even providing financial assistance, to encourage sustainable living, while suburban (and even some rural!) municipalities across the country and trying to make it as difficult as possible (though the regulatory environment in Chicago will be cast in a more negative light in the chapter on commercial kitchens). Whether it is backyard chickens or front yard vegetable gardens, suburbanites have more of a headwind on the sustainable food trail than their city-dwelling counterparts.

The beds were built from 2x12 cedar boards on top of a surface resembling egg crates so as to facilitate drainage. A copper cloth mesh separates that material from the soil to protect the roof from over ambitious plant roots. With the skeleton in place, physics gives way to soil science. There are planting zones across the nation, which are determined by climatic conditions; the zones dictate what can be grown and where. A fully exposed rooftop (that isn't shaded by a taller neighboring building) like the one in this story actually correlates to a different planting zone than the city in which it exists. It's windier, drier, and, due to the warmth coming from the building below, hotter up on the roof. The soil rarely freezes and the growing season is longer. Whereas a typical urban gardener in Chicago might plant the first week of May, these rooftop beds can be planted four weeks earlier. Despite that advantage, many green roofs don't flourish because of the sterile soil environment in the beds; they lack the microbiology that makes the soil supportive of healthy, nutritious plants. It takes fungi to predigest nutrients and make them available to the plants. If the plants can't absorb the nutrients, the plants won't thrive.

For Dave, the rooftop garden was just supposed be something fun to do, but ended up altering Dave's connection with food. Eating in-season requires some thought and planning, and nothing gets wasted. In the future, not even the seeds will be discarded. Dave and Breanne are talking about saving the seeds of plants that demonstrate the greatest potential for the windier, hotter and drier environment two stories above the street. And now that they've shown the way, other city dwellers might recognize that there is an awful lot of unutilized real estate "up there" just awaiting great ideas like this.

## The Foodie

One of Backyard Chicken Run's first customers describes himself as a middle-aged foodie, techie, indie music-listening, gardening, poultry-keeping, libertarian-leaning smart ass. Like the "contrary farmer" portrayed in so many Gene Logsdon books, there is little that Corey can't do himself. Again, opportunities exist both to help people like Corey do what he does, as well as helping people less confident than Corey do many of the things Corey does. (For example, even the most self-sufficient homesteader benefits from a delivery service like Backyard Chicken Run, especially when they are homesteading in an urban environment). He builds pots for tomato plants that water from the bottom up out of recovered 5-gallon food buckets. He builds chicken coops (for anyone that wants help, as well as himself) and rabbit hutches. In the back of a typical city lot in Chicago, Corey has raised rabbits, chickens, turkeys, Cayuga ducks, Muscovy ducks, quail, and my favorite, chukar partridges. This backyard homestead produces eggs and meat, and lots of vegetables to go with it. Corey has had success breeding some of these animals, especially rabbits, the only species he had experience with growing up as a kid in Green Bay. In fact, other than one set of grandparents with a hundred dairy cows (unlikely to make one unique in the state of Wisconsin), there isn't anything in Corey's past that would explain the full spectrum of his efforts to produce his own food in an area measured in square feet, not acres. It started for Corey the same way and for the same reason it started for the chefs and farmers appearing later in this story: superior taste.

It was at a Logan Square neighborhood restaurant where Corey and his partner tried the rabbit gnocchi, "the best taste of food" either of them had ever had. Being skilled in the kitchen, Corey set out to replicate the meal at home. The result, however, was a disappointment. Looking back through the process and the ingredients for clues as to where the mission went awry, Corey found the answer on the packaging for the rabbit meat. It had come from China. Now, I spent a disproportionate percentage of my post-secondary education studying economics, and still enjoy reading things related to economics, such as free trade. For the life of me, I can't figure out why a grocery store in Chicago would have rabbit meat imported from China (see the chapter on distribution and logistics for a few thoughts on this topic). Well, I probably could figure it out, but a part of me really doesn't want to know. Rabbits, as Corey was quick to point out, are pretty inexpensive to rear. And, at the risk of veering off into the unsavory, rabbits are legendary for superior reproductive capacity. A trip to the hardware store and a livestock swap meet later, and Corey was soon raising his own rabbits. Unbeatable rabbit gnocchi soon followed.

Corey's backyard enterprise is as vast an effort as I've seen in Chicago in such a small area. He has had no issue with his neighbors, likely due to the fact that he has at some point cooked a no doubt incredible meal for each one of them, with the primary components sourced just a few feet from his back door. To Corey, good food may start with the taste and quality of the main ingredient, but it doesn't end there. Possessing intimate knowledge of where his food comes from, and how a memorable meal came together, generates not just a positive physical reaction, but an "intellectual appreciation" as well.

Appropriately, given his passion for sustainability, all of Corey's email communications end with a quote from Aldo Leopold's *A Sand County Almanac*. "There are two spiritual dangers in not owning a farm. One is the danger of supposing that breakfast comes from the grocery, and the other that heat comes from the furnace." The quote, from the essay called "Good Oak," goes on to suggest that to avoid the first danger, "one should plant a garden, preferably where there is no grocer to confuse the issue." Corey was confused once; he's making sure that never happens again.

## Today

At Backyard Chicken Run, nearly every delivery day is a study in contrasts. As I drive down to a South Sawyer Avenue customer in the early morning, I occasionally see two prostitutes strolling home after a hard day's night, and other times I drive past lost souls stumbling through a drug-induced haze. Garbage cans lay passed out on sidewalks, vomiting their contents into the street. A fire hydrant left open at the intersection in front of me makes me ponder a different route out of the neighborhood. As I get out of the van to drop the order on the customer's porch, I hear a rooster crow. A second rooster crows, and then a third. I try to get to this neighborhood between 5 and 6 am, after the night owls have gone to bed and before a new dawn arises. Other than noisy roosters, this is a relatively quiet neighborhood, but the streets I need to driver through to get here make me anxious. The three roosters remind me that I've got to keep moving.

None of those three roosters actually belonged to my customer in this neighborhood, Nance Klehm. She is a professional composter, horticultural consultant, landscaper, and public speaker on ecological systems. When it comes to permaculture (the science of modeling agricultural landscapes after natural ecosystems), she practices what she preaches in her own backyard. I don't know the owners of the other three chicken coops on this predominantly Spanish-speaking block in the Little Village neighborhood. It is likely that there are more than four backyard coops on this one block in south Lawndale. One reason is that chickens are iconic to Mexican culture, and today Little Village could also be called Little Mexico. Nance grew up on a farm. She has kept hens for six years in Chicago, and also keeps 15 bobwhite quail. Besides being entertaining, the birds provide Nance with eggs and manure for fertilizer. The Spanish-speaking Klehm says that her neighbors keep chickens for both eggs and meat. Roosters are tolerated in this neighborhood; the males allow the coop owners to reproduce a flock, and help give them fertilized eggs (something these residents prefer to eat). Though there is still some gang violence to tend with in this low- to no-income community, Nance likes living here because she likes living among people that are still connected to the land. Her neighbors brought a wonderful food culture from their homeland: they all cook and possess strong growing and livestock skills. They know their cuts of meat. To paraphrase *Radical Homemakers* author Shannon Hayes, the residents of Little Village treat their homes not as cost centers, but as centers of production. But the long drive to this neighborhood gives me pause. I reflect once again on the diversity of the movement.

Having spent a fair bit of time in Newark, New Jersey, in the 70's and 80's, I have always felt relatively immune to what others would consider "neighborhood risk." Only once since founding Backyard Chicken Run have I been truly worried about my safety, waiting in the van for a customer to open the gate to the fence that surrounded the house while a group of young men sat in a car in front of me, a line of empty liquor bottles on the driver's side curb. I don't know if their day was just starting or ending; I do remember it was seven o'clock in the morning. I called the customer from my cell phone while the rear passenger door opened slightly. A hand came out slowly and added another empty liquor bottle to the curb's collection. The door closed, the engine started, and the car rolled down the street. Exhale, make delivery, and move on. I started Backyard Chicken Run to help people, and this was one of the food deserts that Growing Power's Will Allen and others talk about. Customers living in such an environment don't have sources for healthy food options for themselves, or their pets, nearby. Like Nance Klehm, this customer works in urban agriculture. Backyard chickens are a natural extension of her personal ethos. Her neighborhood feels less safe, possibly more economically depressed, however, than the Little Village neighborhood.

This same day will end with a delivery to a $2.5 million home on Lake Michigan. This customer may share the identical reasons for keeping backyard chickens as the homeowner in the at-risk neighborhood, or may be doing it for a different combination of reasons, I don't know. The point is that both citizens want the right to eat sustainably, to produce some of their own food where the industrial food complex isn't meeting their needs. Both customers want the right to keep backyard chickens (or to plant a vegetable garden, or drink raw goats milk, etc). This particular dynamic, that interest in sustainable eating has no socio-economic boundaries, is one of the most intriguing things about the movement. I cannot tell you what the average customer is like, because I don't think there is a relevant central tendency. Except for age (skewing older than I would have guessed), the demographics of this customer base are all over the map. It's not right, left, nor the middle. It is the whole damn continuum of leanings. My customers include unionized public school teachers and homeschoolers, liberals and libertarians. I have married, single, gay, and lesbian customers, and customers both rich and poor. Sustainable food is *not* a partisan issue, at least not among the voting class.

It is for this reason that I think the accusations of "elitism" levied against the sustainable food movement are somewhat misplaced. At point of sale, certified organic carrots are more expensive than conventional carrots, and therefore out of reach for many low-income consumers. This is irrefutable. But low-income consumers, who possess the same desire for healthy food options, are demonstrating the desire and ability to produce some of this food on their own. They aren't waiting for a Whole Foods to open in their neighborhood. The combination of this effort towards self-sufficiency with delivery services, food trucks, and community gardens, is in effect seeding the market for future organic food outlets. I fully appreciate that Backyard Chicken Run, for example, is "proving" the market for urban farmsteading. Once customer density reaches a certain level in a neighborhood, I expect the local garden center to start offering organic chicken feed and supplies. (This is already happening; Backyard Chicken Run has become a distributor to a couple of retail outlets that can now service some of my former residential delivery customers in the area). So it will be with retailers offering organic food. Delivery services, food trucks, and community gardens will pave the way for greater consumer choice in corner grocery stores.

The Whole Foods shopper should also not be vilified. Although healthy food is justifiably treated differently from other consumer goods by the sustainable food movement (i.e., access to good food should be a basic human right), organic food is still a consumer good. When I press providers of grass-fed beef to explain why their beef costs so much more than corn-fed beef, when grass-fed beef lacks all the industrial inputs, I first get the logical answer: it takes twice as long to grow a grass-fed cow solely on pasture (absolutely true). But when I press more, the rancher is forced to confess: demand exceeds supply. As long as demand exceeds supply (and monopolies or oligopolies are not allowed by regulators), production will increase and costs (i.e., prices) will come down. It is a process; broad proliferation of new and expensive products does not happen over night. The "early adoption" phase is just that, a phase that we must pass through, a phase that always seems to include charges of "elitism." For whatever reasons, the early adoption phase of the sustainable food movement has lasted 50 years. Regardless, we should thank goodness for those early adopters; without them, you will never get to a mass market.

# CHAPTER 5

# A Brief History of "Local"

"Hog Butcher for the World, Tool Maker, Stacker of Wheat, Player with Railroads and the Nation's Freight Handler; Stormy, husky, brawling, City of the Big Shoulders..." – Carl Sandburg, *Chicago*

Chicago is instructive for any metropolis aspiring to build (or rebuild) sustainable food systems because of the city's unique place in the history of centralization and specialization. In essence, The Windy City provides an opportunity to see what must be done, by virtue of what must be *undone*. Centralization and the concentration of market power into the hands of a powerful few are the cornerstones of the "conventional" food system of today. The story of "how we got here" as a country is a story of a shift from small, local, and regional food systems across the nation to one of consolidated market control in the city of Chicago. The prime example of consolidation of power is the evaporation of small, local meat processors around the country. In the first wave of consolidation over 100 years ago, when that meat processing capability disappeared in a local market, the centralized version ended up in Chicago.

**A Brief History of Chicago**

The city's name purportedly comes from a French bastardization of a Native American word meaning "stinky onion." Becoming "City of the Big Shoulders" would take some time, but not too much time.

Providing food, any food, has been big business for a long time. According to historian William Cronon, Chicago's unprecedented growth in the second half of the nineteenth century was a function of the farmers in the country sending the fruits of their labor to market. Wheat was the dominant cash crop in the region. Though farm populations in the Midwest initially clustered disproportionately around St. Louis, the construction of the Galena and Chicago Union Railroad set the stage to leverage one of the most underappreciated inventions in history, the steam-powered grain elevator, which gave Chicago a tenfold cost advantage over St. Louis. This was quickly followed by the creation of the Chicago Board of Trade, which resolved the matter of how the legal ownership of physical grain would be transferred. Standardization allowed grain shipped from Chicago to triple between 1853 and 1856. The next innovation by the Board of Trade, developing a grading system for categories of grain, created whole new markets for the city and allowed Chicago to leave St. Louis in the rear view mirror. Other commodities, such as timber and cattle, followed the path set by grain. Manufacturers took advantage of the low cost of filling the rail cars that would arrive from the west but would otherwise have gone back empty, a key attribute to successful distribution, whether local or global. By 1890, Chicago surpassed Philadelphia to be the second largest city in the United States. The centralizing tendencies of railroads amplified the transportation advantages Chicago enjoyed due to its position between the Great Lakes and Mississippi watersheds. As anyone sitting in today's Chicago traffic jams would agree, "Chicago grew too large, too high-ranked, too quickly."[11]

## A Brief History of "Local"

Before there was a "local" movement there was a movement called "bioregionalism." Bioregionalism is a term that goes back to the beat movement of the late 50's. Though the concept lives (and is gaining strength) in not just the local food movement but also the local *everything* movement, the term itself never achieved exit velocity from the world of academia. If the shop local, make local, and eat local movements were represented as overlapping circles, "bioregionalism" would be at the center of those circles.

How an individual's bioregion, or "home place" in bioregion-speak, is defined is actually *undefined*. It can be defined by topography, geological characteristics, ecosystems, or natural resources. It can also be something cultural. What *is not* used to define a bioregion is a governmental construct such as lines on a map that separate municipalities or bureaucratic entities. Quite often, the watershed is used to define bioregional boundaries. A bioregion, writes Michael Vincent McGinnis, exists at the intersection of culture and community. "These sights, sounds, feelings and tastes are part of my sensual memory of place."[12] Today's "local movement" may have shed the more romanticized foliage of bioregionalism, but its roots in sustainability, conservation, and devolution of power remain firm.

## Cautionary Note on "Local"

I'd like to revisit my earlier definition of "sustainable" as it relates to food: mostly organic, as local as possible. The concept of food security necessarily begins with the idea that consumers can get food when they need it (i.e., when they are hungry). In *Rebuilding the Foodshed*, Philip Ackerman-Leist makes the important point that while the utopian vision of sourcing everything you eat from within a farm within a couple hundred miles sounds great, it represents what most of us should consider an intolerable risk in an increasingly risky world. Whether local climate, economic conditions, or the welfare of the single-source supplier of any necessary input within the local food changes, if one link gets broken, it is necessary to have in existence another source of food supply from outside the region, and a distribution system to access the source. When one sector of the agricultural economy gets hit, writes Ackerman-Leist, virtually everyone involved in agriculture takes some punches. Sage advice ignored at the peril of the local food advocate.

# CHAPTER 6
# The Land of Milk and Honey

"Eat honey, my child, for it is good." Proverbs 24:13

**The Urgency**

It sounds crazy to consider that urban bee keeping might be part of the solution to the problem of colony collapse disorder but the evidence is starting to emerge that it can – and for the very reasons that my raised beds attract bees: an absence of chemical pressure and overall stress. Jeff Leider, of JL Honey, has over 70 hives located on private property (not his own) around Chicagoland. He will not put a hive anywhere near "conventional" agriculture. The reason he gives is simple. He predicts that his bees will die. The bees can seemingly tolerate the heavy and tainted air of the urban core, but can't survive a field of chemically treated, genetically engineered corn. According to author Kim Flottum, "Beekeepers in densely populated urban settings routinely have fewer problems with pests and diseases...losses from agriculture or homeowner pesticides are nearly zero. They lose fewer colonies to *varroa*, *nosema*, and any of the common maladies that beset colonies in more traditional locations. Further, colonies become large enough to swarm and divide more often."[13]

Colony collapse disorder (CCD) isn't the first epidemic threatening commercial beekeepers; the industry has battled the *varroa* mites since 1987. CCD is the scariest, though. It is scary in part because of the speed and ferocity with which it started destroying colonies in the middle of the last decade. The book *Fruitless Fall* follows the history of the disease like a mystery novel, except that this story isn't fiction. One of the earliest documented analyses of recovered bees from a hive crushed by CCD showed that the bees didn't have one disease or another; they had "all of them."[14] The immune system of the bees had collapsed.

What causes CCD? Is it the overexposure to pesticides? Overuse of antibiotics? Genetically engineered crops? Global warming? Maybe trucking bees from Florida to California to pollinate massive amounts of a single crop in one place isn't, I don't know, sustainable. Or is it stress on the immune system due to the entire toxic cocktail? Bees, like another increasingly sick species that shall remain nameless, appear to be nutrient deficient to an extent that prevents them protecting themselves against disease. Eating processed food instead of a diverse, species-appropriate diet of natural food, is weakening the bees' immune system. Perhaps not surprisingly, the high-fructose corn syrup that many commercial bees are being fed isn't solving the problem of nutritional deficiency.[15] The answer, according to a USDA CCD Progress Report from June 2010, was all of the above. Poor nutrition, over-exposure to toxic cocktail of pesticides, and unnatural stressors are together more than honeybees can handle. Our mothers didn't need eight years of medical school to tell us that if we smoked, drank, didn't eat well, and then ran ourselves ragged, we would get sick.

It would be difficult to overstate the importance of bees to our food production. To turn a flower into fruit, pollen needs to be transported, even if inadvertently, from one plant to another. Except in the case of the grains, which use the wind for fertilization, the responsibility for pollen exchange falls disproportionately to the bee. That point was driven home for me on a tour of a hoop house for growing tomatoes year round in northern Idaho. Cardboard box beehives (containing bumblebees, not honeybees) were found in every aisle of the hoop house. No bees, no fruit. So desperate for and dependent upon honeybees is industrial agriculture that the value of pollination services of honeybees now exceeds the market for honey. Even the clover and alfalfa in your cow pastures needs pollination by insect.[16]

### To Bee or Not to Bee

One day it became apparent to me that I was the only one on our block that could grow vegetables in his raised bed garden. Evidently, having a lawn that would make the grounds crew at Augusta National green with envy – as most of my neighbors did - is not conducive to vegetable production. Not using any chemicals on my property, I had plenty of bees (as well as birds and worms). I also had a couple of staggeringly productive raised bed gardens. The bees were not my own, however; the wife is allergic and we aren't sure about the kids.

When it comes to raw honey and bee education, I needed to go elsewhere. One thing I knew from listening to my customers was that bees were quickly becoming the next big backyard thing. This book is not a how-to on keeping bees any more than it is for raising chickens. For that I recommend *Storey's Guide to Keeping Honey Bees* or *The Backyard Beekeeper* by Kim Flottum. The question I was trying to answer is not how but *why* are people doing it and how it might contribute to a sustainable food economy.

### The Hive

I started my investigation with a winter tour of a hive belonging to backyard chicken customer and high school sophomore Kirby Engleman. Whip smart and generous to a fault, she lectured outside on a typically frigid December day at an hour when most teenagers would still be sleeping. Less than a year into her first hive and she had already harvested seven and a half gallons of honey, a prodigious amount by any standard. (Most beekeepers can't extract any honey in the first year of a hive.) I was clearly learning from a beekeeping prodigy. Kirby opened the hive to let me see the bees huddled like penguins at the center of the hive. Then, she walked me through the cycles of bee life and the backyard apiary.

It occurred to me at that moment that I had never seen a bee in winter. Did I think they hibernated? (They don't.) The bees work, keep busy, keep each other warm and fed, and look forward to the spring thaw, just like us. The bees I saw in that artificial hive were both peaceful and beautiful. It's hard to imagine after that brief encounter that many people are afraid of bees.

Beekeeping is a bit of a paradox when compared to keeping chickens. Beekeeping is exponentially more complicated (if you want to understand every element of the miracle that is the life of the honeybee), but actually less labor intensive, once the setup is complete. That complexity is also fascinating. Our cutthroat human politics have little on life in the hive.

The rise of the queen bee to power makes a brawl in the Taiwanese legislature look downright tame. When a colony needs a queen, it produces lots of them. Between two and twenty cells might contain queen larvae, and the first to emerge chews through the side of each remaining queen cell, stinging the pupa inside. If more than one queen emerges at the same time, they fight to the death.[17] A queen might normally reign for 3 or 4 years, but coups are known to happen. If the other females don't like the queen, they won't wait for nature to take its course. Instead, they will lay a bunch of eggs that will be born at the same time, and the new candidates will fight it out for dominance over the hive.

Worker bees, of which there are thousands in a typical honeybee colony, have a rather typical corporate existence. Each female will take on one of six or so tasks at a time, getting promoted through each job. Throughout her career, she will have taken care of the young, built housing, cared for the queen, stood guard, removed the dead (rather unceremoniously, I might add), worked in the heating and air conditioning department, and accumulated the reserves needed to survive the winter. Finally achieving the pinnacle of worker bee life, she leaves the nest to gather food.[18]

After being born without a stinger and living off the good graces of the worker bees for a while, the males, or drones, mature enough to leave the hive looking to mate with a queen from another hive (never their own). Few will be successful, and the ones that are don't live long enough to brag about it; all sex is rough sex for the drone, and he dies right after.[19] Genetic diversity being a strength for the continuing health of the hive (a recurring theme in the sustainability narrative), she takes many lovers on her sojourn abroad. The queen returns to her hive for a lifetime of egg laying (having accumulated millions of sperm cells from this virgin flight), and the surviving drones return to a slothful existence. During economic downturns, the drones are quickly and deservedly deemed expendable by the hive and become the victims of downsizing. Drone larvae are eaten or dragged outside, in order from oldest to youngest.[20] Maybe colony collapse disorder is a function of the deterioration in bee family values, but I doubt it.

## The Honey

As with backyard chickens, each beekeeper might have their own reason or combination of reasons for keeping bees (and each consumer might have his or her own reasons for consuming raw local honey). The two most obvious ones that come to mind are to pollinate a garden, and to produce raw honey. To the extent that pesticides contribute to colony collapse disorder, pesticides are a deterrent to a successful garden. No bees, no pollination. No pollination, no flowering. No flowering, no fruit. (And if you're a professional grower, no fruit, no revenue). Whether or not my successful raised beds are a testament to this belief, it stands to reason. But is raw honey, produced in a backyard apiary, different from what you would typically find on the grocery store shelves? Like other whole foods, the answer is yes.

Honey from different hives tastes different depending on what the bees are using to source pollen. Bees dining heavily on mint will produce honey with a strong, minty taste. Plant your hive next to an apple orchard, and the honey will possess an apple flavor. (It's no different, really, than the impact of different pasture varieties on the taste of grassfed beef or dairy products. You are what you eat.) The mind aches with possibilities!

Is raw honey good for you? Sue Style, in *Honey From Hive to Honeypot*, stays decidedly neutral on the question of the nutritional and medicinal value of honey. Honey generally, already partially digested by the bees, is more easily assimilated by humans than table sugar (i.e. sucrose). If there were good enzymes in raw honey, they would be killed through the pasteurization process that store-bought honey passes through. (The main goal of honey pasteurization, as far as I can tell, is to kill spores that can produce botulism in an infant's stomach, and only an infant's stomach. Thus the recommendation, in either an abundance of caution, or because pasteurization might not kill the spores anyway, that honey consumption is not recommended for infants).[21]

The most interesting potential medicinal benefit that I've heard is not yet covered in the available scientific literature. Some consumers suggest that eating local honey prevents the symptoms of sinus allergies, or hay fever, from developing. The logic is compelling. The bees swap spit with all the local plant life that creates discomfort in the allergy sufferer. Honey produced from the nectar of those same plants might have the properties of an inoculant. Honey from outside the region wouldn't have the same effect. Score one for local honey if the theory ever holds up to scientific scrutiny. If it doesn't, there is always the superior taste, *and* the opportunity to avoid the shadowy side of store-bought honey. Seventy percent of honey consumed in the United States is imported, with the largest supplier being China. Honey from China has been shown to contain everything from banned antibiotics to corn syrup.[22] Regardless, the sustainability score for raw honey is high, because it can be produced locally (unlike sugar), and if kept cool and dry, can be stored for thousands of years.[23]

**The Swarm**

As more and more people become backyard beekeepers in cities and suburbs, the more they – and their neighbors – need the services of people who can get risk of bees who've moved in where they're not wanted – like inside your house. Once that happens, you need someone with both building or contracting skills, and bee skills. In Chicago, that person is Greg Lane.

The problem arises when a group of bees decide to establish a new colony. The "reproduction" process described above is the means by which a colony *maintains* itself. When the bees decide it is time to *multiply* (it's not exactly known who makes the decision), the old queen takes about half the colony with her in what is called a "swarm." That word is as much an action verb as a noun. A swarm is not just a big bunch of bees; it is the biological process by which the colony multiplies. It is an intact colony that sticks together until it finds a new place to start a hive. The bee equivalent of house hunting might only take a few days; find adequate space with a good entranceway, and it's time to decorate. During those few days of exploring and research, it is easy to "catch" the swarm; cut off the branch of the tree the bees are clinging to and drop it in a box. Once a hive cavity is chosen, however, there are only about five days before a colony is established. Bees build colonies *fast*. Getting rid of the bees now isn't called swarm capture; it's called colony removal. Removing a colony requires a completely different set of skills.

Greg Lane's full-time job is still raising his son. But a half dozen times last year he was called upon to cut into someone's home so he could remove and relocate an intact bee colony, all while leaving the building itself the same way he found it. That last step includes removing any honey inside the wall cavity lest it attract a new species of pests. This is not a hobby. The need is growing as more people keep bees, and as the weather warms. The bees are swarming earlier and more often as a result of climate change. Colony removal has proven too sticky a problem for traditional pest control companies. It is too difficult to simply kill an entire colony of bees with chemicals. When it comes to colony removal, there are a million ways to do it wrong, and only one way to do it right.

Colony removal is much more than a potential source of income to Lane. The increasing frequency of swarms has triggered an unprecedented number of complaints to the city. (The "regulation" of backyard aviaries in Illinois is so far limited to the registration one's hive with the Illinois Department of Agriculture). For better or worse, swarms will have a significant impact on public awareness of backyard beekeeping. In that conflict is the potential for education - and a business. Greg believes that honeybees can teach us about the issues of long-term sustainability weaving a thread through this book's narrative, so he wants to see urban beekeeping flourish. Bees can tell us things, said Lane, that no other domesticated species can tell us. They might even get us to reconsider how we interact with the natural world. Honeybees, for example, provide a record of chemical contamination through the pollen they collect and the honey they produce. Either can be analyzed for pesticide content (the pesticides, obviously, having been gathered from local plants within the bees' foraging range). Honeybees have become, in effect, any local food system's "canary in the coal mine." They are more dependent on and sensitive to the health of the environment than humans.

Humans brought the honeybees to North America. There is no "native" honeybee in the United States. Lane summarized the situation for me this way: "Honeybees are a living, breathing scorecard of our impact on the environment. We introduce them to the U.S., we import all of their lethal pests and diseases, we then spread those afflictions to every hive in the country by transporting honeybee colonies from coast to coast for agriculture." The relationship between the two species, humans and honeybees, has become one of mutual dependence; the honeybees need us as much as we need them. Ignore the honeybees and they will disappear.

## The Girl and the Goats

Caroline Ioder (pronounced "Yoder") credits divine inspiration for leading her to the land of milk and honey in the Austin neighborhood on Chicago's West Side. Her salvation from a stretch of chronic boredom came in the form of chickens and bees. Proving the theory that eggs are the gateway drug to the sustainable food movement, the chickens came first. Bees followed in the second year, and by the end of the third year, Caroline had converted her garage into a barn for a herd of six goats.

Though born into the "first generation off the farm," Caroline inherited a pedigree of sorts for dairying. Her father received his Ph.D. in Dairy Science from the University of Missouri, where Dr. William Albrecht, known as the "father of soil fertility research," was his mentor. The dad's specialties were in pasteurization and ultra-high temperature processing, pretty much the opposite of the raw goats' milk for which his daughter is known in urban farming circles.

I made sure I wasn't late for our meeting at Caroline's corner lot near the border of Oak Park. She was planning on taking "the girls" to fresh pasture, a difficult concept to get my head around given the urban locale. (Why all "girls?" Similar to the logic behind keeping hens instead of roosters, females produce milk while males don't. A male goat can be a lot of work to keep around just for periodically impregnating the females, so the males are usually "borrowed" at the time of need from owners on a farm outside the city. Another business opportunity.) From the "barn," we walked through the alley behind a block of homes to a community garden called Root Riot. Here, surrounded by busy streets, Caroline had fenced in several paddocks on land owned by a developer and leased to Root Riot. The developer got stuck with the real estate after the crash in 2008. When conditions call for a change, in an arrangement with Chicago's Park District, Caroline shepherds her goats to the Garfield Park Conservatory to graze one day a week. The goats have become a draw for visitors to the Conservatory, and the Park District saves on lawn care. Occasionally, Caroline sells raw milk or cheese made in a church's commercial kitchen, but the raw dairy is first and foremost for her family. I asked about the potential to turn a profit from fresh chévre. She quotes a bible verse, John 6:35 ("I am the bread of life"), and dismisses any larger ambition. The sales don't add up to much anyway, but the activity helps build a community that is more involved and informed. Questions lead to dialogue, and dialogue to understanding. Mostly, though, this is about herself and her family eating well and living in harmony with nature.

The city is surprisingly hands-off when it comes to goat regulation. As with chickens, Caroline must be careful not to violate the general nuisance clauses (smell, mess, and noise), but as long as she doesn't intend to slaughter the goats, she is on her own. This doesn't mean all her neighbors are enamored with the idea (they aren't), or that they couldn't cause trouble by drumming up a complaint (they have). Caroline has an unusual ally; her next-door neighbor is the ward's alderman. Chicago is divided into fifty legislative districts called "wards," and each ward elects an alderman to sit on the city council. Together, they have the power to license, tax, and regulate public health and safety. If Chicagoans' freedom to farm is going to come under threat, that threat will rear its ugly head via one of the city's aldermen. Caroline's neighbor and alderman embraces this quirky urban farmstead; it's a welcome anecdote to this particular ward's relentless drug-related news flow.

It was Caroline's father's calling to spread the good word of pasteurization around the world. Pasteurization provides two main services to the modern conventional food system. First, the high heat kills pathogens that would be likely to grow in milk the longer the time between milking and consumption (i.e., it extends shelf life and therefore allows milk to be transported over greater distances). Second, pasteurization kills the bacteria introduced to milk by unsound dairying practices; these "bacteria" aren't a function of the milk itself, or the fact that the milk might be raw. This is why in the eyes of author Brad Kessler, over the last century, pasteurization "often became an excuse for dairies to sell, not clean milk from healthy animals, but filthy milk from sick animals whose milk had been cooked clean of its impurities."[24] (Kessler also considers it a truism that great cheese cannot be made from pasteurized milk, thus the reason raw milk cheeses are such a great business opportunity, as I will talk about later).

In his retirement, Caroline's father traveled to an additional fifty countries, upgrading quality control in dairies around the world. Because pasteurization removes the risk of noncompliance with best practices (and the risk from the proliferation of centralized dairies and the subsequent long-distance transport of dairy products) his work likely saved many lives. Caroline's calling was to something different, something older that is new again. Answering the call didn't *lead* Caroline so much; in the end, she brought the land of milk and honey home. Caroline doesn't reject her father's work; she, like many raw milk advocates, merely wants the right to consume the product in what she considers its most natural, and therefore healthiest, state.

# PART III

# The Business of Sustainable Food

# CHAPTER 7

# Pastured Proteins

"But for farm entrepreneurs, the opportunities for a farm family business have never been greater. The aging farm population is creating cavernous niches begging to be filled by creative visionaries who will go in new directions. As the industrial agriculture complex crumbles and our culture clambers for clean food, the countryside beckons anew with profitable farming opportunities."
Joel Salatin, *You Can Farm*

## Barrington Natural Farms

It's 2 AM and Cliff McConville is herding his dozen Black Angus cattle. But he's not on the farm. With the help of a police officer in a patrol car, Cliff is trying to get his beeves (a term used for beef cattle whether male or female) back to the 20 acres he just started leasing from a large landowner. The cattle found a weak spot in the electric fencing and decided to explore downtown Barrington, Illinois in the middle of the night.

Barrington, the reader should understand, is not a country town. It is a town of estates and horse farms 35 miles northwest of Chicago. Cliff, it is also important to know, is not an idealistic 25 year-old beginning farmer. Though he *is* a student of sustainable agriculture. When you hear Cliff's story, you start to recognize another recurring theme. While it is well understood that the average farmer in the United States qualifies for membership in AARP, and young folk are lining up for unpaid internships to learn the ins and outs of organics, there is another demographic with much in common. If fact, there is little unique about the broad brush of my own story: Forty-something, and somewhere in the third decade of a corporate life that somehow should have produced more fulfillment than it did. Or maybe it's that the understanding of what fulfillment means has been plowed under like a failed crop only to come back as something more vibrant, more palatable.

In 2009, Cliff was living on 8 acres with horses and 25 laying hens that he rarely let leave the coop for fear predators would make a meal of the family pets. It was then that the insurance executive and entrepreneur saw the prospects of his white-collar business ventures coming undone by an underperforming partner. The combination of investment losses and disappearing income sent Cliff back to the job market in the only industry he'd ever known. It was about this time that Cliff's sister-in-law, who had already given him a copy of the documentary *Food Inc.* as a gift, followed up with a copy of Michael Pollan's *Omnivore's Dilemma*. Intrigued generally by the insights into how food was brought forth, and specifically by a rebel farmer named Joel Salatin that made an appearance in both stories, Cliff went and purchased Salatin's *You Can Farm*. It was halfway through the book (and halfway to his first day on the new job) that Cliff said to himself, yeah, I could do this.

Back on the suburban homestead, Cliff held the reins of his last horse. The animal was blind and already well beyond the expected life for his species. The veterinarian advised Cliff to take a step back from the animal that stood 16 hands high, just before plunging the contents of two giant hypodermic needles directly into a vein on the horse's neck. Within seconds he was gone, and Cliff was no longer a suit with a hobby farm.

He became a voracious reader, digesting a book a week. He read *Salad Bar Beef* and the next day he was on Craigslist looking for Angus calves. He read *Pastured Poultry Profits* and built an egg mobile to accommodate a new batch of 50 laying hens. He set up killing cones (where the chicken is put in upside down with its head sticking out a hole in the bottom), a scalder (basically a giant pot of boiling water), and built his own tub picker (for pulling feathers) to process broilers on his property. He even picked up six young, 40-pound pigs (known as "feeder pigs"). Cliff named his farm (Barrington Natural Farms) and got a listing on Jo Robinson's Eat Wild website. The reaction was overwhelmingly positive. Due to a combination of that website's well-earned credibility, Cliff's proximity to a large populace, and the insatiable demand for pastured proteins, customers were beating a path to Barrington Natural Farms. (Cliff makes no deliveries as of this writing.)

Disciples of Salatin will recognize instantly that Cliff violated one of Joel's "ten markers for success." Instead of developing one enterprise well before adding others, Cliff was adding product upon demand and now produces eggs, broilers, hogs, grass-fed beef, and raw milk. There seemed to be no end to the demand for sustainable food in this area. Everything Cliff offered on his website sold out quickly. He began the process of leasing 20 additional acres near his home and started calculating how much and how many of each product he would have to sell to provide for his family and give up the corporate life forever. That's when I sat down with Cliff and we applied some basic return on investment analysis to what he was doing.

It wasn't intuitive to me that Cliff should add another 100 laying hens just because he could sell more eggs. So we sat down and modeled what the cost and revenue streams looked like for each product. Cliff had always assumed the egg business was his best business. If you aren't washing or "candling" the eggs (shining a light into the egg to see the condition of the air cell, yolk, and white, and determine if egg meets conditions for Grade A), and the customers come to pick them up, it does seem a pretty nifty business. However, there are challenges to be factored. The farmer has to feed the hens for 6 months before they lay an egg, and still feed them during the molts and slow winter months. If you have to pay your daughter a living wage to collect the eggs, that too would diminish the returns. Lastly, to sell any product off the farm requires another level of cleaning, candling, boxing, labeling and delivery costs that changes the economics dramatically. This is not dissimilar from the regulations surrounding the sale of value-added (baked goods, cheese, etc) through "distribution" (i.e., not direct to the customer from the farm or kitchen). As soon as someone, a store or distributor, gets between you the producer and the customer, food safety regulations become more cumbersome.

Given the high prices, low input costs, and minimal labor required, grass-fed beef seemed like a fantastic business. The problem with grass-fed beef, however, is that it is a working capital hog: Even if the farmer buys the beeves at 6 months of age (for close to $1,000 a piece), you are looking at another 18 months before the animal reaches market weight. (Having to buy hay for the winter at drought-inflated prices is another profit draining challenge, as many in this business came to learn in 2012.) Broilers, however, were a different story.

Broilers, even the pastured variety, require the purchase of increasingly expensive feed. But the cash flow characteristics are fantastic. Eight weeks from chick to revenue. The chickens can be added to the same land as the grazing cattle a few days in arrears. He is maximizing the return on his time *and* land. Even if Cliff thought the beef cattle were superior as a business, maxing out his land with Black Angus would cost him more money upfront than he had to invest. Getting rid of the cattle and filling the pasture with birds would be leaving money on the table (and would require Cliff to run the mower once in a while to keep the height of the grass down). Isn't it fascinating that a sound analysis of the business prospects of different livestock generated the same result as Salatin's theory of mimicking nature on the farm? Birds follow herbivores. Chicken feet follow hooves through the pasture. Chickens break up the cow patties looking for nutrition, enhancing the fertilization of the land. Cooperation. Synergy. Sustainable farming creates a sustainable business. Like nature itself, it's a beautiful thing.

There was one problem with the model. Cliff might be able to sell every pasture-raised broilers he can bring to market, but he can't process them all himself. Organic, grass grazed chicken might be the most underserved market in the greater Chicago area (and I wouldn't be surprised if that were true in most parts of the country). Not because farmers aren't willing to provide the product, but because there isn't a USDA processing facility available in the northern half of the Illinois. A farmer can get an exemption from the state of Illinois to slaughter up to 5,000 birds a year on his property, but when leasing land without access to water and waste management, it becomes a real problem. Most organic chicken farmers in northern Illinois (who either want to process more than 5,000 birds a year, or won't or can't do it themselves) have to drive over three hours south to the town of Arthur to use the services of an Amish-owned and run processing facility. (Non-organic chicken farmers are subject to the same processing regulations and limitations; the organic chicken farmer happens to be further hindered by the absence not just of a processing facility nearby, but one that is processing only "certified organic" broilers). Grow the birds locally, but drive 400 miles round trip to bring them to market. That's not the picture of sustainability. Local capacity to process livestock (beef, pork, and poultry) is a *key* piece of the sustainable food network puzzle. Unfortunately, it requires more than just access to capital and adventurous entrepreneurs (both already in short supply as it relates to the sustainable food industry). Regulations and an understandable "not in my backyard" mentality form a barrier to the construction of new livestock processing facilities. One potential interim solution I see is to have some of the small livestock processors already in existence expand their capacity. Chicago actually has a USDA inspected facility (USDA inspection is necessary to sell across state lines) right in the city. Few farmers know about it because the owner has been processing primarily chickens from his own farm for nearly three decades. Still, Ciales Poultry may be the hidden jewel of the local food system in Chicago.

## Perez and Ciales Poultry

On my second drive down to Ciales Poultry, my thoughts drifted to a trip through Spain 20 years earlier. In a small town outside Madrid, I stood inside a 900 year old building whose architecture and carvings betrayed its mixed heritage. In different parts of its history the building had been a mosque, a temple, and a church. When I toured the Ciales Poultry processing facility the week before, I saw labels on boxes of broilers that stated not the customers' names, but what can only be described as the cultural preference for how a bird is slaughtered and processed. Halal. Chinese. Buddhist. (There is no "Christian" tag. Christ, radical Rabbi that he was, subordinated dietary law and rituals to other demonstrations of commitment.)

Here in a processing facility masked by a modest store front, cultures from around the world once again come crashing together, but at the same time, not just the same place. I was here to sit down with the owner, Raul Perez, and his business development head Manuel Bey, to talk about how much Ciales Poultry would charge to process birds for a third party like Barrington Natural Farms. The business Mr. Perez had built over the last 31 years happened to be vertically integrated. The chickens he was processing all came from his farm 2 hours away in Milford, Illinois. This humble man in the white butcher's coat (who Mr. Bey, no spring chicken himself, calls Papa) was both the keeper of millennia old traditions and a potential hero in the local food movement in Chicago.

Raul Perez emigrated from Cuba in 1969 at the age of 23. He worked for Westinghouse Electric for 11 years before seeing an opportunity to provide the kind of fresh food that nourished him as a child to the different cultural communities in Chicago. Raul acquired the current facility in 1980.

Today he ships his birds all over the country. I am told that there is interest from China. Processing according to Islamic law is actually performed by an imam in Raul's facility. A prayer is said (or thought) before the chicken's throat is slit. The head is left on. Raul slaughters for the Buddhists and Chinese communities, leaving the feet attached as well. The Chinese prefer a hen to a rooster. The requirements of halal specify not only the ritual of slaughter, but that the animal be treated with respect and well cared for. Raul's chickens, you see, range freely on pasture.

Although we aren't in the market to buy his finished product, and although my Spanish still wouldn't be sufficient to hold a dialogue with Raul even if he didn't speak a Lowland Spanish dialect, we speak the same language when it comes to food. Restaurants and consumers want local pastured broilers. Farmers in the suburbs of the city are ready to provide the product. Processing is the missing piece of this particular puzzle.

And Raul knows it. In trying to negotiate a price for processing hens for local farmers, several challenges became evident, some specific to the Ciales operation. First, as stated earlier, Raul has his own farm and his primary business is processing his own chickens, a system that occupies both his facility and a USDA inspector two days a week. To add a third day for the benefit of local farmers is going to require a minimum number of birds likely to exceed one thousand (for that one day). Raul would have to bring in both a small crew of workers for that day, and a USDA inspector (the specific dollar amounts were not disclosed for competitive reasons). You would be hard pressed to find a farmer within two hours of the city (of Chicago, but I suspect it's true of other cities) that could produce broilers in 1,000 bird batches. That, therefore, requires yet another layer of cooperation between multiple farmers (another business opportunity!).

The net of this first pass at negotiating with Raul on behalf of local livestock farmers (which I did primarily as an advocate for local food and farmers) was a prohibitively high price per bird for processing. At least, it seemed prohibitively high when compared to the price of the Amish processor down south, before travel time was taken into account. Because he is generous to a fault, Raul still sent me home with one of his broilers. Some clarity to the issue of Raul's processing cost per bird was hanging from the plastic bag in my hand. The broiler was at least seven pounds (compared to 3 to 4 pounds for a "typical" organic or pasture-raised local broiler). If the financial analyst assumes a sale price of $4-$5 a pound for an organic, pasture-raised broiler, Raul's higher processing cost per (much larger) bird no longer seems prohibitive. Not that it costs more to process a bigger bird. It doesn't. Which is why I'll make the prediction that sustainable broiler sizes will get bigger. I have heard many a sustainable farmer declare that the livestock community slaughters its animals sooner than would optimize flavor. It might also be true that we slaughter the animals sooner than optimizes profit to the farmer. The resistance will no doubt come initially from the customer, who, farmers tell me, prefers a sub-4 pound broiler. Still, price per pound as well as taste will dictate that broilers will get bigger.

# CHAPTER 8
## Raw Milk

"The simple truth is that you can't make top-quality cheese from pasteurized milk...Pasteurization incinerates the building blocks of good cheese – the *lactobacillus* indigenous to the milk. It also destroys the aromatic esters...from the plants the animal's been eating, which give raw-milk cheese its unique herbal flavors, its *terroir*.
– Brad Kessler, *Goat Song*

When Cliff opportunistically picked up a couple of Guernseys, he couldn't have anticipated just how quickly selling raw (that is, unpasteurized) milk would be a great business. It is now the cash cow of his operation. Moreover, raw milk is necessarily (for regulatory reasons) the ultimate local food business. Every state has its own regulations and restrictions, but in Illinois, raw milk is legal to sell only if the customer comes and picks up the milk on premises (at the farm). You can't deliver raw milk in Illinois. (The primary concerns with the sale and consumption of raw milk generally are the time between milking and consumption, the number of hands the milk passes through, and the distance the milk travels from farm to consumer. Selling direct to the consumer off the farm addresses each of these in some way, even if to varying degrees). At $10 per gallon, and in spite of the fact that Cliff supplements the cows' pasture grazing with some organic no-soy dairy feed, each Guernsey is generating several hundred dollars a month in profit. Why such strong demand? Like eggs from backyard hens, every customer has a different combination of reasons for wanting raw milk.

After the "safety" issue (covered below), the potentially superior nutritional content of raw milk is the next most hotly debated topic. One of Cliff's customers, Dan, drives thirty minutes each way once a week to get raw milk in part because he believes it cured his young son's dermatitis, an inflammation of the skin commonly caused by an allergic reaction. The skin around the boy's joints was "raw." The dermatitis, which hadn't responded to steroid creams prescribed by the family pediatrician, vanished after two weeks of drinking raw milk. If Dan failed to make the trip to Barrington Natural Farms and his son drank pasteurized, store-bought milk, the dermatitis returned. In truth, Dan can't say that the raw milk *cured* the dermatitis; it's possible the pasteurized milk was causing it, and in its absence the skin condition went away. What he *does* know is that he could turn the dermatitis on and off like a switch depending on which milk his son drank. Needless to say, all in the family are now committed consumers of raw milk.

Other customers want the "good" bacteria and enzymes that can only be found in raw milk (pasteurization, proponents of raw milk contend, kills anything living in the milk, including good bugs). Raw milk from grass-fed cows is more nutritious, containing more vitamins and good fatty acids than pasteurized milk. Milk purchased direct from a farmer (pasteurized or not) offers the customer an opportunity to consume dairy without contributing to a system of food production the customer finds offensive (i.e., confined animal feeding operations, large corporations dictating price to powerless farmers, etc). Some customers believe raw milk is easier to digest (because it still contains the enzyme that aids digestion, an enzyme that is killed in pasteurization). And last but not least, there is the superior cheese that one can make at home with raw milk.

## Regulations

The state-by-state regulation of raw milk ranges widely. As of this writing, farm sales are legal in 18 states, and retail sales are legal in 11 states. The "cow share" model (where a group of individuals are deemed the legal owner of the cow, and the group pays a farmer to milk the animal) is an option in at least 8 states. Raw milk can be purchased as "pet food" in 3 states. Everywhere else it is either outright illegal, or prohibitively difficult to navigate the regulations (i.e., you can drink raw goats milk on a Wednesday under a full moon with a note from your doctor). It's especially important to emphasize "as of this writing" because regulations are constantly in a state of flux. The state of Illinois provides a timely example (again, as of this writing). There is a move afoot to make the regulation of raw milk so onerous as to kill the nascent industry. To avoid a legislative vote, the attackers (I dare not make specific accusations, as they would be exceedingly difficult to prove) have worked through the Illinois Department of Health to redefine the rules. The rules would require a combination of licensing, inspection, and limits to production that would render the venture into raw milk financially unsustainable. The "cow share" model should remain an option for farmers (that would require a vote of the state congress to undo) that endeavor to persevere. But as a sustainable food business, the trend in raw milk regulation in Illinois is not the farmer's friend.

If drinking milk generally comes with its own controversy, raw milk is downright alien. Whenever I bring up Cliff's success with raw milk, I first get asked the question, "Should we be drinking milk at all?" Lactose tolerance, after all, goes away around age 5 in most humans[25]. The story is more complicated than that, however.

In 1939, Weston A. Price, DDS, published a book called *Nutrition and Physical Degeneration*. He had traveled the world researching isolated populations eating indigenous diets, from Swiss villages, to African tribes, Australian Aborigines, and residents in South Sea islands. As a dentist, he focused on studying dental decay caused by nutritional deficiencies. What he discovered was that those same nutritional deficiencies promoted disease beyond the teeth and gums. He paid particular attention to milk.

What he observed were diets that were by definition "bioregional" in composition. Milk was consumed by the nomads of the Arab world (camels milk in this case), Asiatic peoples (milk from sheep and musk ox), and the residents of Swiss villages, because it was the most nutritious source of sustenance available. This native diet supported excellent dental and overall health, especially compared to the victim of a highly processed western diet. He made another discovery relevant to this book: an animal on a poor diet, such as grass grown in poor soils or grain, produced milk deficient in nutrition.

According to biologist Rob Dunn, evolution for western Europeans living with milk producers favored the gene that produced lactase (the enzyme that breaks down lactose) nine or ten thousand years ago. Whatever the trials and tribulations of the time, a human possessing the gene to digest lactose was more likely to live long enough to pass on that gene. Those that couldn't tolerate drinking milk, were less likely to do so. Thanks to my Germanic roots, I get to enjoy milk and cheese without incident, while others are less blessed. Roughly 25% of adult humans can't tolerate any lactose, while another 40-50% can only partially digest it. [26] Statistically speaking, lactose tolerance is still an evolutionary trait that puts the owner in the minority.

Opponents of raw milk preach from the pulpit of health and safety. It's strange, that a source of sustenance that allowed tribes of people to survive and pass along their genes to their ancestors would be considered today to be hazardous to one's health. To be sure, many people in the 19th and early 20th century got sick and died from drinking raw milk. They didn't die, of course, from the milk itself. They died from certain bacteria in the milk, the product of either the living conditions of the animal or poor handling of the milk. The cow's feces coming into contact with either her udder or the milk is the most obvious example of a source of contamination that will make someone sick down the trail. That is particularly likely in the event a cow is confined to a small space and reduced to standing in its own waste. To read Robert Hartley's description of the urban dairy in the 1840's is to read a time traveler's review of the modern confined animal feeding operation:

"If the wind is in the right quarter, he will smell the dairy a mile off; and on reaching it, his visual and nasal organs will, without any affection of squeamishness, be so offended at the filth and effluvia which abounds, that still-slop milk will probably become the object of his unutterable loathing the remainder of his life. His attention will probably be first drawn to a huge distillery, sending out its tartarian fumes, and, blackened with age and smoke, casting a somber air all around. Contiguous thereto, he will see numerous low, flat pens, in which many hundreds of cows, owned by different persons, are closely huddled together, amid confined air, and the stench of their own excrements. He will also see the various appendages and troughs to conduct and receive the hot slush from the still with which to gorge the stomachs of these unfortunate animals, and all within an area of a few hundred yards."[27]

Note the references in the above passage to both the living conditions of the animal and the animals' diet (i.e., waste from a distillery). As I see it, pasteurization was a reaction to the vulgar conditions and dairy practices of the time. A cow that alternately walks or lies in grass most of the day is less likely to transmit fecal infection, but requires a cleaning before milking just the same. To expand on a theme started earlier in this chapter, the inherently limited shelf life of milk does not lend itself to the centralization of milk production and its subsequent long distance distribution. To expand on yet another theme throughout this book, pasteurization, like other innovations used extensively in the conventional food system (i.e., food processing, the use of preservatives, etc.), doesn't benefit the taste or nutritional content of the product. Pasteurization extends shelf life, accommodating (with help from refrigerated trucks, of course) the transportation of milk across the country.

Raw milk is out of necessity a local product, and a great *local business* as a consequence.

Some states that license raw milk dairies require periodic testing. Illinois does not (yet). Cliff, though not boastful by nature, tests his milk every six weeks, and the results are something to crow about. Of the two tests that commercial dairies are required to use, the Standard Plate Count (SPC) is the most important. Simply stated, it's an overall measure of bacteria colonies in the milk. A commercial dairy can let this number run close to 100,000 "colony forming units" (cfu's) before running afoul of regulations. Even a commercial dairy should be able, with best practices, to keep this number below 10,000 cfu per milliliter of milk. High counts indicate a few possible problems: dairy equipment that has not been sanitized properly, inadequate cooling, mastitis (a mammary gland infection), or "poor production problems" (i.e., dirty cows). Over the second half of 2012, Cliff's cows averaged less than 1,500 cfu/ml.

The Raw Milk Institute (a certifying body for raw milk dairies) recommends a second standard. The coliform and *E. coli* test is a proxy for unsanitary production practices or mastitis infection. Counts as high as 100 cfu/ml are considered acceptable in the industry. In the last six months as of this writing, Barrington Natural Farm's two highest coliform results were 20 and 10. He's never shown any traces of *E. coli* 0157:H7. (There are hundreds of strains of *E. coli*, and most of them are harmless to humans. This one, 0157:H7, is toxic and increasingly showing up in America's conventional food system).

## Making Cheese

Even if drinking raw milk is not on your bucket list, making cheese is a cottage industry worth watching. I had the good fortune to speak with "The Cheese Queen" Ricki Carroll about the market. Ricki said sales at her New England Cheesemaking Supply Company exploded after she and her company were mentioned in the 2007 release of Barbara Kingsolver's book *Animal, Vegetable, Miracle*, and never looked back. In operation now for over three decades, demand for her home cheesemaking kits is still skyrocketing.

Some of Ricki's home cheesemaking customers have graduated to the professional ranks. As with raw milk, every state has its own rules for selling cheese generally, and selling cheese made from raw milk specifically (check your own state's regulations before trying to make and sell cheese). In the state of Illinois, cheese made from raw milk need only be aged for 60 days to be legal for sale. For someone like Cliff, who has customers bringing their own containers to his farm to pick up gallons of raw milk, turning any of the high-priced milk in to cheese might not be worth the extra effort. (Estimates vary depending on the kind of milk used and cheese being made, but it generally takes well over a gallon of milk to make a pound of cheese. Someone like Cliff would therefore need to charge a hefty price per pound to justify the extra time needed to produce cheese from milk that can already be sold at a high return on investment). It's a different story if you're more than an hour away from a large customer base.

Ninety miles northwest of Chicago, a stones throw from the Wisconsin border, a farmer had just such an epiphany. Eight years after starting a CSA with three other partners, Ron is the last member still farming. Despite putting in 16 hours on some of the hottest days in memory last summer, the business is still just breaking even. There wasn't enough time left to market the CSA after being "all things" to his existing members. Though still considered "local" to Chicago buyers, the transportation costs to participate in those farmers markets are prohibitive for his small operation. But right in his backdoor, a Rockford, Illinois restaurant owner fell in love with the taste of Ron's raw goats milk cheese. So much so, he offered to buy all the cheese Ron and his small herd of milking goats could produce. This is the kind of value-added business opportunity that increasingly represents the difference between a struggling family farm and a financially viable farm business.

There are a lot of dull red barns and gray silos between the greater Chicago area and Ron's homestead. His ranch home, protected by weeping willows on either side, sits not too far off the county road. The diversity of the farming operation, a stark contrast to the surrounding monoculture, can be seen from the driveway: gardens, hoop houses, a chicken coop, and a barn for the goats. During my visit, the family dogs, Zoe and Cole, let us share the comfortable sofa chairs in between a wood burning stove on one side of the sitting room and a five-gallon bucket of fermenting home brew on the other.

If you held a gun to Ron, I'm guessing he would say that eight years ago he was a university professor who did some farming on the side. Eight years later, he is a farmer who, like most in the business of growing, has an "off the farm job" teaching music to supplement his income. His restaurant customer is begging for mozzarella. Ron dreams of raw milk gouda. Not so much that he becomes a billionaire, but just enough to "pay the bills," and put a little aside for the golden years.

Ron is the first person to vocalize what I've been thinking for over a year now. The word "sustainable" wasn't invented for either the environmental movement, or the organic food movement. The business community has always used the word to measure a company's ability to exist without having to borrow money from a bank or sell equity to investors to pay its bills. Ron's business, though break-even, isn't really sustainable. One more drought, one more big bill for hay, and the farm will be in the red. The solution, as many small farming operations are finding, may be to "forward integrate" into value-added products. One example of forward integration would be going from selling milk to a large cheese manufacturer (that buys from lots of dairy suppliers) to becoming both a dairy and a cheesemaker. As another example, Ron's wife would like to make organic, frozen quiche with the eggs that currently don't command a price (in rural Illinois) by the dozen that justifies having layers and giving them organic feed. For his part, Ron, encouraged by the enthusiasm from local restaurants, wants to expand his goat herd and start making cheese from the raw milk.

But regulations pose some challenges to this business plan. Though Ron could sell the milk right off the farm in the state of Illinois, he can't sell the cheese unless it's produced in a commercial kitchen. The same of course would go for his wife's quiche. "We're legalizing marijuana, and criminalizing eggs and milk," he laughs.

Not surprisingly, there is no commercial kitchen out where he lives, and Chicago is too far away. His goal, to build a commercial kitchen on his own property, would cost $10-$20,000. Adding in a milking parlor would cost another $5,000. But he knows it has to happen. Forward integrating into value-added food products is for many small farmers the difference between subsistence and sustainability. Create a real brand name in the process, and "Katy, bar the door."

Fortunately, so desperate was the restaurant in Rockford for Ron's cheese that the owner offered his restaurant's own kitchen to Ron for free. His cheese is the best in the area by far, something Ron attributes to the quality and diversity of the pasture he seeded himself: a mix of alfalfa, three different types of clover, and three different types of grass. The connection between the animal's diet and the food it produces is poetically described by Brad Kessler in his book *Goat Song*: "cheese so young and floral it held within its curd the taste of grass and herbs the goat had eaten the day before. It seemed we were eating not a cheese, but a meadow." With raw milk, Kessler argues further, each cheesemaking is different from the last; the components in the milk change day to day.

Ron knows he has to eventually make the leap of faith, expand the herd, and build the kitchen. But will someone make the leap of faith with him? He doesn't know if a natural lender or investor exists in his neck of the woods. If not for the financial hurdle, and the fear factor, it would be an easy decision for Ron. He talks about returning his garden beds to pasture and leasing another two-acres from a neighbor as if it is a foregone conclusion. Then, instead of working 16-hour days on his vegetable CSA, he can milk once in the morning and make cheese for five hours. That would also leave time for marketing and bookkeeping, tasks that quickly get put on the backburner after long days in the field. Cheese making has other advantages. Cheese can be stored and shipped; unlike milk, it doesn't need to be consumed right away. Human's milked goats for thousands of years before tapping the first auroch, ancestor to today's domesticated cow. This is one reason goat's milk is tolerated by more people than cow's milk. Why Ron's raw-milk cheese *tastes* better might be the same reason the eggs from my backyard coop taste better. To quote Kessler again, "Every raw-milk cheese is an artifact of the land; it carries the imprint of the earth from which it came. A cheese - even a fresh chévre – is never just a thing to put in your mouth. It's a living piece of geography. A sense of place."[28]

# CHAPTER 9

# Celebrity Chefs

"How we eat can change the world." – Alice Waters, Chez Panisse Founder

I am a connoisseur of nothing. I walk into a restaurant like Inovasi in Lake Bluff with great trepidation. I was surprised how much on the menu appealed to a knuckle-dragger like me. So much so that I ordered four appetizers instead of an entrée because I simply couldn't choose. Everything was delicious. I was especially impressed with the items I'd never heard of before, like quinoa balls. Candidly, I had no idea what a quinoa was or that it even *had* balls. What I did know before sitting down was that Chef John des Rosiers had constructed the entire menu with ingredients from sustainable sources. When I left that night, I couldn't wait to talk to des Rosiers and find out why. He would answer the first question of our interview a month later with a single word: taste.

It all starts with taste; just being local isn't enough. Soil types and acidity levels impact what can and should be grown on a farm. A mismatch will show up in yields and taste. The cattle from his beef supplier graze in a pasture populated with over a hundred species of grass and plants. If the cattle eat just one kind of grass, the meat will taste, well, grassy. Give the cattle access to what Joel Salatin refers to as a "salad bar" for herbivores, and the result is unparalleled flavor – just as with pasture-raised goats and their milk.

The result is really a different product entirely from corn-fed beef for more reasons than just taste. Grass-fed beef cooks 30% quicker and therefore requires different preparation technique. The dynamic caused by variable taste and shorter time on the grill is a hurdle for broad adoption of grass-fed beef; one bad experience at the higher prices this meat commands and a consumer is less likely to come back for seconds. This is an example of why chefs can play such an important role in the adoption of sustainable food. Chef des Rosiers doesn't just make his grass-fed steak sizzle, he makes it sing.

The value-added doesn't stop there. The Inovasi menu lists all the major suppliers to the restaurant right at the top. After a memorable dining experience, a guest is apt to look up those suppliers and buy some product directly. I know I did. It is more than one way, then, that a sustainable chef can both pull and push sustainable food through a local market. Not only does the chef bring out the superior taste of local food, but he or she contributes to local food market growth by connecting the consumer directly to the farmer. This in turn helps the farmer grow and increase the likelihood that the farm can continue to supply this particular restaurant, and hopefully others. Thus, providing sustainable food also becomes a sustainable business.

So why doesn't every restaurant limit itself to sustainable ingredients? Because it's harder to do. Because it requires a flexibility that most restaurants lack if they weren't created from the ground up to source from 35 or 40 different vendors. Because it's easier to make one or two phone calls when you need something than it is to accept dozens of small deliveries every week. It's also more expensive. On average, buying sustainably in this way costs des Rosiers 30% more upfront. A sustainably produced tomato costs more than a mass-produced, chemically laced tomato, and the additional logistical challenges of buying from so many different vendors creates its own set of additional costs. (These additional costs are mostly labor related. Compared to mechanized, conventional agriculture, sustainable agriculture creates jobs not just on the farm, but beyond as well).

By opening his restaurants in the suburbs instead of the city (where customers are used to paying much higher prices for good food) he significantly raised the degree of difficulty for his business plan. Built more for the defensive line than the cooking line, des Rosiers doesn't come across as someone that is easily turned back by challenges. Bringing this quality fare to the suburbs is intentional. It's part of a business plan that stretches out over decades. This is a very long-tail opportunity. This trait, this strain of conviction, may be what separates des Rosiers from the pack more than anything. The same is often true of great investors.

As a chef working his way up at Trotter's, Gabriel's, and Bank Lane, des Rosiers simply wanted better *food*. Forty years earlier and 1,500 miles away, Alice Waters wanted the same thing. Her credo was fresh, local seasonal, and wherever possible, organic. That sounds a lot like the definition of sustainable food that is gaining traction today.

Like the bumblebee that aerodynamically can't fly but doesn't know it, Waters had not a scintilla of experience that would have justified a foray into entrepreneurship when she opened Chez Panisse in Berkeley. More accurately, she knew it but didn't give a damn. Unlike the French chefs she idolized, Waters had no local distribution system for the basic ingredients she wanted. Her years of building a local food system included not only shopping farmers markets, but also actually foraging for watercress, fennel, and blackberries.[29] Candidly, eating seasonally in California isn't quite the challenge it is in Chicago, or other latitudes above the 40th parallel. In addition to the climatic differences, Chicago lacks the local food network that now exists in Northern California. Both facts are problems, but they're also business opportunities.

Chef de Rosiers described to me the service that would make his life easier. It was a distributor that would aggregate his orders for locally produced food and bring it to him once a day, instead of thirty-five times a week. He even envisioned using the Green City Market, Chicago's largest farmers market, as a food hub for breaking down and allocating restaurant orders; the farmers were already coming in to the city twice a week for the farmers market. In a local food economy, every foodshed would need each of the many different components described in this book, though the components in a metropolis like Chicago would likely look very different than the same components in a rural area. The larger the city and surrounding areas will differ in another regard; "knowing your farmer" gets increasingly difficult with the size of the local market and distance (and layers of distribution) between consumer and producer. In some ways that's not terribly different from the national food system that provides most of us with most of our food. The solution may be yet more third party verification, entrepreneurial websites (such as the equivalent of Jo Robinson's Eat Wild website for products and services other than pastured protein), or the expansion of customer-driven review sites into sustainable subject matter (i.e., restaurant reviews where the reviewer brings clarity to the "sustainability" of a restaurant's menu).

## Uncommon Ground

I've always envied people who seem never to have questioned what they would do with their lives. There's no wasted time or energy. Every effort seems to move the person forward. Great things inevitably happen as a consequence. Something great happened in Chicago around New Years 2013, when a restaurant in the Lakeview neighborhood was designated the "Greenest Restaurant in the Country" by the Green Restaurant Association. It was the second time in three years for Uncommon Ground; the newer location on Devon Avenue won the award two years earlier. If that wasn't enough, the Devon Avenue restaurant also features the nation's first Certified Organic Rooftop Farm. With all the accolades, visionary proprietor Helen Cameron became what you might call an overnight sensation, twenty-two years in the making.

Unlike the other characters in this story who ventured into unknown territory in midlife to participate in the sustainable food movement, Helen grew up with "foodie parents." The differences between her father's Chicago address and her mother's farm downstate weren't as drastic, from a food perspective, as one might expect. Wherever she went, there were fruit trees and currant bushes. The family grew food organically because it was the only way they knew how to do it. Store-bought fertilizer was never an option financially; composting was just naturally part of the growing system. An abundance of apricot, cherry, and apple trees on the two homesteads provided ample opportunity for this self-described "city mouse, country mouse" to practice the now nearly lost art of canning. The experiences of her youth informed every part of what she has done in the restaurant business.

The time Cameron spent studying chemical engineering at Purdue was her only substantial excursion outside the world of food that I can see. That educational experience was cut short when her mother fell ill. Helen moved back to Chicago to finish school, but started working in restaurants right away. By the time she was twenty-one, she had already done everything there was to do in a conventional kitchen. Her childhood experiences and memories would eventually influence her direction as a professional restaurateur. In 1991, Helen and her husband opened the first Uncommon Ground in what was then a modest storefront. Through three expansions since inception, the restaurant consumed more and more of the corner at Clark and Grace. Another expansion, to add a microbrewery, is already planned for installation in 2013.

Just as the physical space has grown incrementally, so too have the efforts that led to the Greenest Restaurant award. Sustainability may have been on Helen's *mind* from day one, but not everything was possible immediately if the restaurant was going to succeed. You do what you can, Helen insists, "as you can afford to do so." Otherwise, the business *itself* might quickly become unsustainable. As mentioned previously, the word "sustainability" is used in the business world to measure a company's capacity to survive without outside funding. In that sense, Helen's genes may also have played a part in her success as a restaurateur; she believes she inherited her frugality (and commitment to cleanliness) from her German mother. The two award-winning restaurants grew out of these values, *and* two decades of "reinvesting everything back into the business." To put it another way, Helen set out to create a sustainable ecosystem with her restaurants. It was an evolutionary process that didn't happen overnight. When it came to sustainable food, Helen chose to fight the battles in the order that she thought was most important.

From the beginning, Helen shopped the farmers markets. She learned to incorporate those cherries from the Michigan farmer into her menu when they became available. Perhaps most important to her, however, was local meat production. Uncommon Ground can now source all of its protein regionally. She takes on only a couple of new farmers a year because of the time required to teach and train them how to service a restaurant like Uncommon Ground, which now serves up to 22,000 meals a month between the two locations. Helen wants the mission of each farm she works with to be aligned with the mission of Uncommon Ground. That, she says, is more important than organic "certification."

For Uncommon Ground to remain a going concern, the farmers who supply it must also exist on more than life support. It's quite a balancing act. The farmer needs a fair price to survive, and the customer demands a fair price to make a dinner reservation. The restaurant gets to perform a complex balancing act in the middle. It requires chefs that are committed to sustainability, and exceptional training and communication between the kitchen and farm. Moreover, sustainable food sourcing requires a lot of research up front, costing, and recosting, all with an eye on the menu mix. Lastly, the model demands particular attention to how items are portioned, which helps keep waste to an absolute minimum. Performing this balancing act well is the "secret sauce" at Uncommon Ground.

As soon as Helen saw the big open sunny roof space at the Devon location, she immediately thought of growing food up there. Her husband agreed. It just seemed like common sense to use that space productively, which for a restaurant meant growing food. Now Helen grows tomatoes, peppers, cucumbers, corn, eggplant, peas, beans, fennel, Swiss chard, kale, potatoes, garlic, shallots, spinach, mustards, arugula, and a wide variety of herbs and edible flowers. "We really want biodiversity on our farm as it is part of organic practice." The farm doubles as a "school" to teach many people about urban agriculture. The farm employs a full-time salaried director, a part-time assistant, and up to seven interns over the course of the growing season. The farms go well beyond the idea of being a "good business." The farms inspire everyone who comes in contact with them, changing lives for the better in the process.

Efforts to decrease the environmental footprint of the restaurant didn't stop with buying or producing local food. Uncommon Ground has made significant investments in energy savings. Energy savings can be then be reinvested in to either more energy saving initiatives or in to *food*. It is a misconception that being green is always more expensive. Nearly every green initiative has saved Uncommon Ground money. The solar panels on the roof paid for themselves in a little over three years. Savings on electricity were reinvested in hand dryers, which cost Helen three thousand dollars between the two restaurants. Subsequently, a thousand dollars a month in paper towel savings resulted in a quick payback and extra cash to buy LED lights. The lights were saving the restaurants five hundred dollars a month as soon as they were turned on. The additional electricity savings allowed Helen to spend a little more on composting. It also gave here the flexibility to work with new farms and educate them about how to supply a restaurant like hers.

The result is the greenest restaurant in the country, and one that sources food locally about as well as it can be done. The Green Restaurant Association (GRA) has seven "Environmental Categories" of which sustainable food is just one. Each food item is ranked on its certified organic status and food miles (the distance from farm to restaurant). When it comes to the percentage of food that Uncommon Ground sources sustainably, Helen's scores "blow everyone out of the water." The GRA considers "local" to be within 100 miles, and everything within 300 miles to be "regional." Nothing compares to her "farm," which is how Helen refers to the rooftop raised beds on Devon and the earth boxes that surround the restaurant on Clark. Together they produce 1,000 pounds per year of food.

# CHAPTER 10
## Commercial Kitchens

The economic barriers to starting a food business are high and growing higher. The "commercial kitchen" is so many great things at once. It is an incubator for small business. (In fact, in addition to being known as a commercial kitchen or shared-kitchen, this model is often referred to as a "kitchen incubator"). It is a joint venture between investors and entrepreneurs. It is also new territory for regulators.

### Kitchen Chicago

Alexis Leverenz cannot lay claim to having inherited more than a passing interest in food. Not only did she lack any interest in *cooking* food, she rarely thought twice about *eating* it. That is except for a curious obsession with buttercream. Her petite presence is enough to create some doubt as to whether or not she has ever tasted either butter *or* cream. Doubt vanishes, however, when she begins to wax poetic about wedding cakes. Still, it's a big leap from frosting a cake to running one of Chicago's surviving commercial kitchens.

Alexis left the Detroit area for college and an investment banking job in Chicago's Sears Tower. It was work, but not a vocation, and twelve years ago she started to think about a second career. Alexis chose the aforementioned buttercream creations over the income potential of future in computer science; she enrolled in a French pastry school. Starting over in any new field comes with its own harsh realities. In her case this meant long hours scaling ingredients and doing dishes for minimum wage. While working in other people's kitchens, she realized she was either going to have to make a business out of this on her own, or go back to investment banking. Like a lot of people starting out in the food industry with a low tolerance for risk, Alexis thought to use the kitchen in her house first. Unfortunately, in Illinois (and I'm guessing many other places) you can't legally sell something to the public that you baked at home. At that point in time, there were some commercial kitchens elsewhere in the United States. These facilities were primarily government-funded or non-profit organizations in low-income neighborhoods focused on job training. There was nothing in Chicago designed to help Alexis with her local food venture. There were, however, a lot of other people looking for a similar resource from which to build businesses out of baked goods. The city obviously needed a for-profit commercial kitchen. Alexis decided to seize the opportunity.

So she began to search for a location. It would seem that that the easiest way to get a commercial kitchen up and running would be to buy a restaurant that was going out of business. Unfortunately, retail banks looking to expand kept getting there first (purely for the prime real estate; the banks weren't getting into the restaurant business). Finally, Alexis found a commercial kitchen that was going out of business and for $30,000 she was able to takeover the location. That was February 2005. The only food license available at the time that came close to serving the needs of a commercial kitchen was the Retail Food Establishment License. Two people in the city's licensing department gave Alexis *verbal* confirmation that she could operate a commercial kitchen under this license structure; no one in the city's licensing department, Alexis and others would learn, ever gave any answers in writing. Perhaps naively, Alexis marched forward with her business plan based on those verbal blessings. Business was conducted in this manner for four more years before it came time to look for bigger space.

## Logan Square Kitchen

Across town, another food entrepreneur was not having the same success navigating Chicago's web of regulations. By the time I made the trip to see Logan Square Kitchen (LSK) founder Zina Murray, her five-year odyssey through start-up hell was coming to an end. LSK was founded as a commercial kitchen, a place for food artisans to grow and prosper through that awkward stage between home and wholly owned operation – the kind of service Ron and his wife could use to build their cheese- and quiche-making businesses.

It started with the purchase of a building on the 2300 block of North Milwaukee Avenue. The untrained eye can't see so everything that makes the building special. One of the many goals in Zina Murray's detailed business plan was to make sure the building was Gold LEED certified. In addition to the shared kitchen, Zina's business plan required that the building would also support an event space; both businesses would be necessary to support the building's mortgage. (Alexis, on the other hand, was always a tenant, subleasing space within a larger building, which provided better flexibility than owning a whole building, especially a Gold LEED certified one).

Zina's personal story should possess some familiar tones by now. In midlife, working as a consultant after 16 years in advertising, she happened upon an opportunity that she thought was important for the community in which she lived. Having seen several grocery stores in Logan Square close, and an organic food chain attempt and fail to open a store around the block, Zina realized that there was little in the way of food security in her neighborhood.

Like others in this story, her zeal for good food in her personal life was about to become a professional pursuit. There was nothing frivolous about her concern for good food. In her early 30's, she became sick with a host of illnesses related to an endocrine system collapse. She had been allergic to the food she was eating day in and day out. As her condition worsened, she decided to pull the parachute on her traditional healthcare providers and pursue nutrition as an alternative source for both the cause and the cure. With the help of a clinical nutritionist, Zina regained her health and vigor. Over a decade later, in August 2007, she bought the building on North Milwaukee Avenue that would become Logan Square Kitchen, hoping to assist the kind of local food producers who had helped her get well succeed in building sustainable businesses.

Nearly two years after that, just a few months before the kitchen's scheduled opening in September 2009, Zina hired a "license expeditor" to navigate the process of acquiring business permits in the city of Chicago. Having reluctantly caved years ago to paying someone to prepare my tax filings, I have to say it is disconcerting to think the process of acquiring just the *licenses* to start a new business is so onerous that an industry has sprung up to guide you through the maze--for a fee. There is a whole industry of professional services in Chicago with the sole purpose of getting things done at city hall. This is a business opportunity local food promoters probably wish didn't exist. But it does.

Zina and her expediter decided to first pursue a Retail Food Establishment License, the same license being used at Kitchen Chicago. The plan was rational and straightforward. By getting one license, the kitchen would enable each of its customers (vendors that used the facility) to operate legally without having to go through the licensing process themselves. It was apparently working for Kitchen Chicago, though no one had ever gotten direction from the city in *writing* as to whether or not this structure would pass muster.

At first everything seemed to be going fine. Logan Square Kitchen received its Retail Food Establishment License and then applied for a liquor license and public place of amusement, or PPA, license, for the event side of Zina's business model. Seven different city departments came out to inspect the facility. That was the beginning of the end. Logan Square's application did not pass the Business Affairs requirements; the location of the tables in the dining area did not match the location of the tables in the drawing submitted with the original application. Actually, the tables weren't there at all. Zina hadn't worried about it because there was no reference in the city code to floor plan conformity. Still, Zina explained that the location of the tables might change due to special events (receptions, corporate outings, or any private parties). Business Affairs rejected the application anyway. At a future date, Zina put the tables back in the dining area as they had been depicted in the application, and Business Affairs granted its blessing, conditionally, for the PPA license.

Unfortunately, the department had changed the building's "use determination" (literally, what the building would be used for) that had been in place since Zina got a building permit two years earlier, from a "restaurant" to a "banquet facility," and the city required banquet facilities to provide far more parking than retail food establishments. But there was no room for that much parking in Logan Square. Zina Murray had a license contingent upon conditions that could just not be met in her neighborhood. Zina took her appeal to the Department of Zoning, or what she refers to as the "fifth circle of hell." Unfortunately the Zoning Board simply refused to even consider overruling the licensing department's findings. Meanwhile, the nascent shared-kitchen business started to add customers operating under the one Retail Food Establishment License for the Milwaukee Avenue location. At this point in the process, every new retail food establishment license application from a new kitchen user was accompanied by a health inspection by the city.

**Things Come to a Head**

Alexis moved Kitchen Chicago into her new larger space on Leavitt Street in September 2009, about the same time that Zina was opening LSK. By early 2010, applications for a Retail Food Establishment License could be completed and filed online. The combination of a much less onerous application process (compared to going downtown and waiting in line) and positive press surrounding Alexis' new space, produced a flurry of online applications for Retail Food Establishment Licenses using the same address on Leavitt. This brought Kitchen Chicago (not just its customers) directly to the attention of the city's licensing department generally, but specifically the attention of a health inspector on a mission. Alexis was anticipating a health inspection related to two new applications when this health inspector arrived and immediately issued cease and desist orders for all Kitchen Chicago customers (on the grounds that, at this point, a retail food establishment license only accommodated one business per physical address). But that wasn't all. The agents started to throw out all the food in the walk-in freezers, declaring that it had been produced by unlicensed vendors and was therefore unfit for human consumption. The kitchen was treated like a crime scene; the walk-in freezer doors were covered with tape and warnings against opening. Take anything out of there, said the inspector, and you will be committing a crime.

After a few well-placed phone calls from Alexis, NPR, Monica Eng of the Chicago Tribune, and other news outlets rushed to the scene. The aftermath of the raid played out over multiple days. As nauseating as the experience was for Alexis and her customers, the *city* was the one that got the bad press (i.e., the reporters covering the event cast the city in a negative light). *This* is what it took to bring the city to the table in a productive way. Within a couple of months, the city officially agreed to allow multiple retail food establishment licenses at a single location. This was no panacea, mind you. For each Retail Food Establishment License issued, a health inspection was still performed. For LSK, the net result was nineteen inspections over two years, rather than the 2-4 per year required by a traditional restaurant. Moreover, how burdensome the inspection was for the shared-kitchen owner was a function of which individual city health inspector showed up. For Zina and LSK, that inspector was usually the same inspector that had performed the raid on Kitchen Chicago. Each inspection was performed as if the inspector had never been in the building before. When Zina complained to a health commissioner, that inspector was moved out...to the licensing department. There, he proceeded, according to Zina, to make it exceedingly difficult for her potential kitchen-user customers to get licenses to work in LSK, if they got them at all. Now, neither side of LSK's business model was moving towards sustainability.

Not long after "the raid," Logan Square Kitchen hosted recently elected Mayor Rahm Emmanuel for a press conference, at which the Mayor announced a plan to reduce the stifling number of business licenses in the city of Chicago from 117 down to 49. Zina contends that the license requirements that eventually went away were for licenses that were rarely if ever used, and that food-related license requirements have not gone down in Chicago. Moreover, if the bureaucrats behind the 49 licenses end up being the most intransigent of the bunch, entrepreneurs might not see the improvement. Nonetheless, in May of 2011 (more than a year after the raid on Kitchen Chicago), and with the help of the Industrial Council of Nearwest Chicago (a small business incubator and advocate) and other support groups, a peaceful resolution was reached. The result of a half dozen meetings was a new set of licenses designed specifically for commercial kitchens. One license, a Shared Kitchen License, was created for the owner-operator of the kitchen itself. The other, a Shared Kitchen User License, is only $330 for two years, and a short-term license (90 days) is available for only $75. These modest fees are important for two reasons. First, the original Retail Food Establishment License was prohibitively expensive for the individual tenant, making it difficult to launch new businesses. Also, the commercial kitchen is really intended to be a bridge for food entrepreneurs, not a place to set up and stay forever. The User license is also *transferable* to any other licensed commercial kitchen in the city (to the extent more are ever created).

## Conclusion

LSK did not survive despite the new licensing regulation. Zina did, however, reconfigure a city building, allow food entrepreneurs to start businesses, taught clients how to work in a sustainable kitchen, and helped those clients find places elsewhere when LSK shut down. In the end, the building became the second unit of a vegetarian restaurant chain called Chicago Diner, so at least the people living in Logan Square ended up with more access to good food, as Zina had hoped they would.

It would not be difficult to conclude, with the advantage of hindsight, that despite paying for professional guidance through the licensing labyrinth, mistakes were made during the launch of LSK. It's also not difficult to conclude that those initial missteps should have been easily overcome, if it were not for what Zina describes as suffocating bureaucracy, vindictive public employees, and intractable incompetence. These problems were baked in to the process from the beginning because there was no code for commercial kitchens at the time. This is another example of the need for new regulations to encourage, rather than discourage, the kind of institutions and opportunities needed to build a sustainable local food system.

The benefits of the commercial kitchen compound exponentially. An entire new industry, the food truck industry, will be able to grow and prosper much more rapidly than it otherwise could have because of the existence of the commercial kitchen (at least in Chicago; food trucks can't actually cook in the vehicle). In the early years of Kitchen Chicago, the business was built almost entirely on cupcakes. Now food trucks are the fastest growing segment for the Kitchen. (Though food truck regulations in Chicago can hardly be described as supportive of growth, but that's a developing story). If helping to tangentially launch another entire segment of the local food economy wasn't satisfaction enough, Alexis gets to watch her customers expand, mature, and eventually leave the nest. It is a long and growing list of branded food-related companies that got their start at Kitchen Chicago and are now big enough to justify their own space: Bleeding Heart Bakery, TipsyCake, 5411 Empanades, Hoosier Mama Pie Company, Blue Sky Bakery, Katherine Ann Confections, and Pasta Puttana, just to name a few. Some now have multi-million dollar facilities. Even in its short time in operation, several sustainable food businesses got their start at LSK, including Jo Snow Syrups. Three other LSK clients went off to share their own new kitchen space. *Top Chef* winner Stephanie Izard hosted two "Wandering Goat" dinners at LSK before opening her now famous Girl & the Goat restaurant.

The efforts of not-for-profit shared kitchens focused on workforce re-entry are socially vital, and I hope they are replicated across the country. But to transform this nation's trillion-dollar food industry, there should be more than a handful of commercial kitchens in a city the size of Chicago. Until that time, food entrepreneurs can look into churches that often have licensed commercial kitchens that might be available for rent on an hourly basis.

The commercial kitchen is in a way the epitome of growth in the importance of "local" over organic. One individual commercial kitchen has the power to help launch dozens of other food-related companies. If that isn't something local regulators can get behind, I don't know what is. Like our backyard chicken regulations, I hope municipalities across the country emulate these more liberal regulatory frameworks as the green initiatives that they truly are.

# CHAPTER II

## Pet Food

I am convinced that many of the business opportunities that exist in the sustainable food movement for humans also exist in the world of pet food and supplies. Those opportunities, though smaller in size, will still include local food, organic food, logistics, third party verification, and even commercial kitchens. And why not. The issues driving the movement for sustainable human food (i.e., physical health and well being, environmental health, healthcare costs, animal welfare, etc.) are all mirrored in the market for pet food.

When my boxer Max sat next to you, he always leaned in just enough to initiate physical contact with your lower leg. It wasn't a display of dominance that would have drawn criticism from our dog trainer. It was only Max's need for affection behind this behavior. He deserved that opportunity because like most dogs, Max gave ten times more than he received.

You often hear people talk about how "human" their dog seems. Max definitely displayed what seemed to be a full range of human emotions: excitement, enthusiasm, sadness, compassion, loneliness, and love. But that's different in a subtle but important way from saying he was really human because Max lacked guile. He could tease you and taunt you, but there was no dark corner in Max's heart, like the dark corner that exists in all of us. Max was so gentle, I used to say, that he could take a single Cheerio out of my two-year old son's fingers without getting them wet.

It was two weeks from the time I first noticed Max was having issues moving his bowels to the time the veterinarians diagnosed him with lymphoma. What started out as a couple of lumps high on his neck just below the jowls had spread like wildfire throughout his body.

I hear all the time how people, especially empty nesters, refer to their dogs and cats as their children. I have been guilty of drawing the same comparison when talking about Max. I know it's not the same thing; though serious challenge and tragedy remain conspicuously absent from my life, I am not without perspective. As a parent, there is nothing I can imagine more awful or wholly unnatural than being predeceased by a child. Pet owners enter the relationship knowing they will bury their dog or cat at some point. Not that this makes it easy in the end.

The scientists at the animal hospital wanted to cut Max up and flood him with chemotherapy. "We're having lots of success these days treating lymphoma." No, he was gone. I wouldn't have chosen that path for myself at this point. I wasn't going to put Max through it for a *de minimus* chance of surviving, no less thriving. I felt my only obligation at this point, as his friend and caregiver, was to make sure he didn't suffer, and he didn't die alone. It certainly wasn't an issue of money; the day before the symptoms started I dropped three thousand dollars, cash on the barrel head, to save Max's left eye from a bacterial infection eating its way through the cornea. In fact, I initially thought the early cancer symptoms were just a hangover from the surgery, maybe the anesthesia. Wishful thinking.

The steroids that I'd been told would give Max a couple more pain-free weeks had the intended result for only a couple days. Convinced it would be uncomfortable at best, and painful at worst, to move and transport Max, I begged our veterinarian to come out to the house and put him to rest. I felt fortunate to have a vet willing to do that.

I stretched myself out on the floor along Max's back as he lay on his side, cradling his neck so his head rested on my upper arm. I whispered into his ear, which realistically was probably more of a comfort to me than Max. I never looked down at his feet where the doctor was doing her work, but I could tell by listening to Max's breathing where she was in the process. Still, it was a jolt when his breathing stopped, and my heart broke. For the first time in two weeks, I didn't have to worry about Max's care. Two years later, I'm still saying goodbye.

Max had never been to the doctor in between annual checkups. Then, at just five and a half years old, he was gone. I started to research what might have gone wrong with Max. I started to dig in to the world of dogs, and I discovered two things. First, Max was a pure-breed boxer. I'm sure, as in every profession, there are good breeders and bad breeders, more inbreeding and less. Regardless, the lack of genetic diversity in a pure breed dog sets them up for almost predictable health problems down the road. You can research, by breed, and see the ailments the pure breed dog experience: joint disorders, heart disease, and susceptibility to cancer, to name a few.

The second thing I discovered was that the plague of chronic diseases in the human population was being mirrored in the world of domesticated cats and dogs, including allergies, obesity, diabetes, and cancer. I contend that the reason is the same: our companion animals are not eating a healthy and species-appropriate diet. To be familiar with Michael Pollan's *Omnivore's Dilemma* and William Davis's *Wheat Belly* is to know that the human condition is being diminished by the dominance of corn and wheat on grocery store shelves (at the expense of whole foods like vegetables, meat, eggs, fruit, and raw nuts). To be familiar with America's system of agricultural subsidies is to know that those grains are artificially cheap, to the benefit of large food processors and the detriment of consumers. Not surprisingly, more than a little of the pet food on the market is being stuffed with subsidized grains, like corn and wheat (I can't say exactly what percentage, but the biggest brands are the biggest practitioners of grain stuffing). If "conventional" corn and wheat should be no more than a small part of the human diet, it should be even *less* a part of the diet of a dog, and none of a cat's (dogs are technically omnivores, as their ancestors would likely have eaten the stomach contents of the herbivore hunted and killed for dinner. Therefore, some healthy, unadulterated vegetables can show up in quality dog food. Cats are purely carnivorous). Flip the bag of dog food from a big box retailer or grocery store over and more likely than not, you'll see corn and wheat on the ingredients list. Sadly, there are some formulas listed as "organic" that are made with grains that while grown to certified organic standards, still have no place in your pet's bowl.

Why share this personal story in a book about business opportunities within the sustainable food movement? Just as the disease trend has developed in parallel (in humans, dogs, and cats), so has the health food trend. In fact, I think the pet food world is ahead of the human food world. In some ways, we feed our pets better than ourselves. How many times have you heard a caring pet owner instruct a child not to give that breaded and fried chicken nugget to Fido, because "that's not good for him." The trend is to feed a species-appropriate diet to the animal. Specifically, the theory is to go back and imagine what that animal would eat if it still lived in the wild.

There are two other parallels between the pet and human worlds to consider, both under the price versus value umbrella. First, if you give your dog or cat a higher quality, species appropriate feed, the dog or cat needs to eat less of it. So the higher price you pay per pound of the food doesn't mean a dollar for dollar increase in your pet food budget. Second, though health insurance is beginning to creep into the market, most people still pay veterinary bills out of pocket. A little more money up front for higher quality dog food might save you a small fortune in vet bills down the road. Sound familiar?

Another affliction increasingly common in humans and showing up in dogs is allergies. No one can tell me the cause yet. It seems logical that the cause would be environmental, as I believe it to be in the case of humans. Is it leaky gut? Meat sourced from livestock fed genetically modified grains? Or is it the result of a trend over the last decade or more towards keeping a pet on a single formula for its entire life. I don't know fore sure. I do know that pet food allergies are having an increasing effect on the dog and cat side of the Backyard Chicken Run business. I am constantly being told that an owner's dog is allergic to chicken or beef or some other staple protein. The solution, I'm convinced is more organic dog and cat food, and more diversity in the diet. Though there is an abundance of "grain-free" dog and cat food, "organic" pet food is still pretty rare, and locally-made pet foods are rarer still. Just as in the market for human food, these are all great business opportunities.

The "local" theme is also increasingly present in the pet food market, with its own teachable moments. I cannot, at any price, sell a pet treat made in China to my customers. Whether it is all true or not, the blogosphere is filled with stories of dogs getting sick or worse on this or that treat made in a Chinese factory. As discussed in the section on greenwashing, add this to the reasons "local" is becoming more important than organic: You can import (or export) organic, but you can't import local.

Do we have animals because of the unconditional love they give us? Or because we are made to feel good through the care and comfort we provide to them? The explanation for why over 60% of homes have at least one pet is usually stated as the former, but when I think of the hours I spend rubbing my dog's belly or scratching him behind the ear, I start to think it's more of the latter. People need and appreciate help in caring properly for their pets. That's a recipe for a good business.

# CHAPTER 12

# Farm to Fork Logistics

## The Home Delivery Movement

There is a natural growth curve for organic food growers. No one crawls out of the crib and sells to big food distributors. Something has to come between CSAs and farmer's markets on the one hand, and selling to large institutions on the other. Big customers inherently bring big risk and challenges as well as big volume. If Cliff McConville of Barrington Natural Farms ever wants to expand his business beyond "off the farm" sales, or Ron wants to grow his raw milk cheese business beyond a couple of nearby restaurants, a new, local food distribution network needs to evolve in northern Illinois. For food entrepreneurs like Cliff and Ron, the network needs to evolve everywhere. One natural interim partner is a direct-to-home grocery delivery service, structured specifically to handle fresh produce from local organic farms. Chicago is lucky to have one of the nation's innovators in this business.

### Fresh Picks

There is a repeating thread in the fabric of this local food story. I didn't go looking for it, but it keeps showing up, demanding attention. Like other local food entrepreneurs, Irv Cernauskas and his wife, Shelly, were in the third decade of their corporate careers when they both found themselves ready for a change. Irv had been a self-employed information technology consultant, and his wife a banker. Having always possessed a keen interest in mission-based businesses, Irv wanted a second career that would advance his environmental and social goals, while also giving him direct daily contact with people he liked and respected. To the benefit of sustainable eaters in Chicago, this reevaluation of lifestyle preferences and personal values led to the creation of "Irv and Shelly's Fresh Picks" in 2005.

After a year of planning and investment, the company started aggregating orders for fresh vegetables, meat, dairy, and other locally grown grocery items, delivering them directly to homes across the city. The industry exists at the confluence of two powerful secular trends. First and most obvious is the trend towards eating sustainably produced (mostly organic, as local as possible) food, the main subject of this book. The second is a reversal of the 20th century trend toward increasing dependence on the automobile. This may not be true everywhere, but in Chicago you can live without a car. There is ample, affordable public transportation, and a large and growing commitment to bike lanes. Not all of the carless are young. The aging population would rather have heavy goods brought into the home (and might also have more disposable income than a younger demographic). Going out, finding parking, hauling big bags from the store to the car and then again from the car into the home, become less attractive with age. Since demography is destiny, this trend (assuming it *is* a trend) only looks to get stronger.

The behavior at the younger end of this barbell is the one that surprises me; I take the press at its word that it even exists. Teenagers and young adults today are not in the rush to get a drivers license and buy a car with the same enthusiasm I felt when I was coming of age. Enthusiasm isn't strong enough a word. I think I was in front of the Department of Motor Vehicles, waiting impatiently for them to open their doors on the birthday that made me a legal driver. *Owning* a car would have to wait, but only for economic reasons. Having access to a car was equivalent in my mind to having freedom. Freedom today comes in the form of the Internet, and from *not* having a car payment. I personally think it's a far superior way to live, and it benefits the environment tremendously. Car ownership is incredibly expensive, and we now live in the age of austerity (another secular trend). Getting rid of car payments, insurance, registration, parking, gas, maintenance, and repair is a financial windfall.

Moreover, if you need a car, you can now rent one by the hour, a service that didn't exist decades ago. Even if you need a car for a week, it's quite affordable and convenient when spread across a few travelers (compared to everyone flying). As an aside, car rental agencies can't help but benefit. Once resident primarily at airports, new car rental offices are opening city and suburban locations. Like any retail business, the agencies' new "stores" are following the customer.

For farmers, Fresh Picks is not just a convenience; Irv's company is a necessary business partner. I am aware of so many farmers and food artisans who own their own delivery trucks and run routes that just can't be optimized for profitability. The trucks run only a couple days a week and come home empty, the epitome of underutilization. As an environmental advocate, Irv at first had reservations about adding another vehicle to the already crowded streets of Chicago. But his service takes hundreds of car miles a week out of contention for precious asphalt.

The customer experience is superior to going in to a grocery store in a few ways. The food is better and no more expensive than what a shopper gets if he or she gets in the car and drives to a big box organic food store. And, it's more convenient because the food is brought directly to the customer's door. Currently, a Fresh Picks customer's delivery options are limited to only certain days of the week. I expect that to change in a way that creates a virtuous cycle of growth for Fresh Picks. The more dense the delivery route, the closer to need Irv can deliver the order, the more customers find the service compelling, and the more efficient delivery becomes again. This would address the number one reason Irv doesn't serve half the population of Chicago already; people just aren't planners, especially when it comes to meals.

This home delivery model has other societal and economic benefits. There is little waste in a small and relatively flat farm-to-fork food chain. There are a few reasons. If you don't think a delivery service can bring produce to your door that would look like something you would pick out of a bin from the grocery store, you need to think about how the traditional system works. For something like a tomato or apple to get from a farm to your shopping cart through the traditional network, at least a dozen hands will touch it (including more than a few of your fellow shoppers). In Irv's model, it's just a couple hands doing so. The farmer picks and packs the produce, Irv puts it in your box, and you are the next and only other person to hold it. This not only increases the likelihood that produce shows up unmarred, but might also diminish the odds of contamination caused by passing through so many pairs of hands. If a tomato looks like it might fail to meet customer standards, it becomes a Fresh Picks employee perk. If even one of the warehouse crewmembers wouldn't eat it, the tomato goes back to the farmer for on-site composting. Zero waste. This is a vast improvement over America's global food distribution system that sends at least thirty percent of our agricultural production to the landfill. And the customer doesn't need to contact each farm or walk a farmer's market to source a plethora of local food. He or she just orders from Irv's website (where the customer can also see what farm provided each product). Irv and Shelly's Fresh Picks is a consolidator for your orders, and sits like the narrow neck of an hourglass between dozens of farmers on one side and thousands of customers on the other.

The opportunity has not been lost on potential competitors, who are starting to crop up. Every new venture brings with it a new angle on how the model should evolve. Fresh Picks and its direct-to-home competitors all still have to compete with traditional brick and mortar retail. At least the food-to-home service providers don't have to compete with Internet retail in a meaningful way; that beast has a large and growing presence in the market for pet food. Competing against both Internet and big box retailers has shaped my view of how any home delivery model might work best. I have to look at what strengths the local home delivery service possesses versus big box retailers and the Internet. I hope this discussion stimulates some useful ideas for boutique retail grocery and pet supply stores necessarily offering delivery services to compete with Internet retailers. The economics of local delivery are very similar for both the warehouse in the suburbs and the storefront in the city.

Whether customers aren't good at planning or they just have a need for instant gratification, speed is of the essence. This is especially true with the more youthful side of the demographic barbell. Most local delivery services have opted to require customers to accept a single delivery day each week in order to maximize the profitability of the service at the outset. As I said about Irv's business, as it is with any delivery business, the clusters will eventually become dense enough to justify "next day" delivery as an option for everyone. I have taken the "build it and they will come" approach and offered next day delivery to everyone in my delivery area. It's one less reason for someone *not* to use my service. I fund slightly higher fuel and labor costs in the interim, but give the business every possible chance to gain new customers *today*.

Another piece of the home delivery profitability puzzle is minimum order size. Both mail order and home delivery services that offer free delivery need to ensure that an order is big enough to be profitable. But "big enough" only means total price, and that is a dull instrument when it comes to measuring profitability. What matters is the gross profit (the difference between the cost of the product to the retailer and what the retailer sells it for) on the order, regardless of the size of the sale, and every product has a different gross profit margin. Ideally, a web ordering system would start with a delivery charge and work back to zero based on the gross profit in the basket, offering popular or related items that might help the customer *get* to free delivery. This functionality is still in the development stage for my business.

The third piece of the puzzle, and the one with the most potential for delivery services to compete with both Internet and traditional retail, is related to *total* order size. In theory, pricing should be structured to share the benefits your business gains from larger orders with the customer. The way I look at Internet retail, the delivery cost is fixed per bag of food, and therefore goes up with each and every additional bag ordered after the first (i.e., the *total* shipping cost *varies* with the number of bags ordered, but is a *fixed* cost for each bag). At the risk of getting bogged down in semantics, the total shipping cost can therefore be described as *variable* with *fixed components*. Whether it is UPS, Fedex, or the U.S. Postal Service, every thirty-pound bag of dog food costs a set dollar amount to ship. An Internet retailer just needs to make sure that the gross profit on each product is slightly higher than the cost to ship that product. In contrast, a brick-and-mortar retail has a delivery cost that is relatively fixed in the form of monthly rent on the building (or a mortgage if the retailer owns the building). That retailer needs to continue selling product at whatever price and margin will generate enough total gross profit to cover the cost of the building and the people working in it.

The home delivery model is a unique hybrid. I, too, have a fixed cost, but my fixed cost is the trip (gasoline and time) to your door (the warehouse cost isn't as cheap as the warehouse an Internet retailer sets up in the desert, but it's also not as expensive as the store in the city). I need to make sure that the minimum order size has a gross profit that covers *that* fixed cost. I'm not going to underprice any competitor on the first bag of kibble. The second bag, however, is a completely different story. Assuming the gross profit on the first bag of pet food covers the fixed cost of the delivery, every extra dollar of gross profit falls (from any extra bags), as they say, to the bottom line. No one should be able to beat me on the price of the second (or third) bag. Most retailers offer a delivery service now. No retailer on Main Street should lose out to an Internet retailer on orders with multiple items. This is the main reason I see the pet food delivery business skewing to the "heavy users" (i.e., big dog and multiple pet households).

For a few reasons, it's a little more complicated than that. Any delivery vehicle has a fixed amount of cargo space. When I look at the empty space on my delivery van I see gross profit dollars per square inch. The bulkier an item is, the less attractive a delivery item, all things being equal. Moreover, because space on the vehicle is fixed, there is diminishing return to offering additional products at a lower profit margin to the same customer. At some point, I need to put a full priced product (or two) in the next available spot on my van. But you get the point. I know this opportunity is not lost on existing, peripheral players that all want to migrate from legacy business models to the local delivery opportunity. Local logistics companies and messenger services call me regularly with the suggestion that I sell my van and let them make the deliveries for me. From different directions, Internet-based and brick-and-mortar retailers all striving to provide same day delivery. I summarize these competitive forces in the chart below:

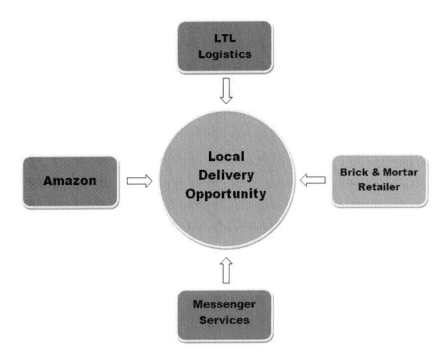

Lastly, I believe some Internet retailers sell product at a loss to drive competition out of business. They use the profit from one business segment to subsidize losses in another. That's a heck of a headwind for even well constructed local strategies. There has been much in the press lately about the "hall pass" on sales tax collection for Internet retailers (without a presence in the particular state in question) finally coming to an end. Until then, local retailers need to offset that structural price disadvantage with the personal touch and superior service that can only come with direct interaction with customers.

There are other competitive strategies that have been used in traditional retail for decades. They center mostly on offering something proprietary, something that no one else can offer but you. Until you have that, all retail quickly becomes a commodity business. Nothing much will matter, however, as long as Internet retail businesses don't have to collect sales tax. Trying to save customers a dollar here or a dollar there is nothing in a city like Chicago where the sales tax is over 10%. I think it is well understood how destructive Internet retail's free pass on sales tax is to local economies (in states that depend on a sales tax). What I *don't* think is understood is how insurmountable the sales tax arbitrage is to the ability of local business to compete. The higher the ticket, the more pronounced is the absolute savings to the consumer that avoids local sales tax. Consumer electronics is the most recent example; that local retail trade has been just about vanquished.

## Upstream Logistics

Internet retail and sales tax aren't a problem for the local system for human food, however. The single most limiting factor for the local food system is, according to Irv, what he calls the upstream logistics. If it doesn't make sense for farmers to be making home deliveries in company trucks, it doesn't make much more sense for them to be driving from their farms to commercial customers in the city such as Fresh Picks. There is still a truck depreciating behind the barn two or more days a week. That money is better spent by the farmer on another tractor or hoop house. And the farmer's time is better spent farming than driving. Yet right now, there aren't a whole lot of options for a farmer an hour or two away to get the harvest to town, at least not in Illinois.

Neighboring Wisconsin has a well-developed network of "less-than-truckload," or LTL, carriers that specialize in shipping small freight. Those carriers also have fleets of refrigerated trucks, critical for moving perishables around. Maybe not coincidentally, the Badger State has the second most certified organic farms in the country, second only to California (though the size of the average farm in California is much larger). As a consequence, Fresh Picks gets more organic food from Wisconsin than Illinois.

The local market doesn't need a high-tech, web-based exchange where buyers and sellers can find each other. Go to the Green City Market or the Evanston Farmers' Market on any summer weekend, and you will likely collect the business cards of every organic farmer within a two-hour drive of Chicago. What the market needs are LTL carriers and *food hubs*. A food hub means different things to different participants in the local food movement. To Irv, a food hub need not be anything more initially than an aggregation point. It is a warehouse with a loading dock to store local food under proper conditions with easy access just off the highway. It is at least twice as expensive for a farmer to bring his produce into the city in his own truck, and bring it home empty, as it would be for a large carrier specializing in keeping its trucks full in both directions. I source my organic poultry feed from Cashton, Wisconsin, over four hours away. A third-party carrier brings a pallet of feed to me for about $70. It doesn't require a calculator to see that I couldn't come close to saving money trying to do it myself; either the fuel or the eight hours of labor would exceed the charge from the LTL company. Keep your core competency in house and outsource what you can of the rest.

Some organic farms have been acting as food hubs for the providers in the region. In Wisconsin, Harmony Valley Farms already had trucks from third-party carriers coming to its loading dock when it invited others to participate in the network. Mike Callicrate, proprietor of Ranch Foods Direct in Colorado Springs, uses his beef processing location (his cattle are across the border in Kansas) in similar fashion. Other small farmers in the area now bring their goods to Mike's warehouse where they load product on the same trucks that are bringing Ranch Foods Direct meat into and around Denver. The Ranch Foods Direct location also doubles as a CSA pickup point for everything from meat and vegetables to raw milk. There's more than enough business for everybody, and the diversity of produce has led to a retail farm store at the site. Longer term, the food hub can add processing and packaging, and not just for vegetables. Callicrate has partnered with Renewable Harvest to add a mobile meat-processing unit to his local food network. He's also partnered with Pikes Peak Urban Gardens to bring manure into the city for soil amendment.

## Shippers versus wholesalers

This local market opportunity is not lost on the traditional food wholesalers; they already have refrigerated trucks making deliveries all around the local market. The biggest industry players have even created subsidiaries with different names than the parent company. They possess the wherewithal to be more involved in solving the logistical challenges described above, but at a price. I see a growing tension between the two options, wholesale distributors and LTL carriers. Traditional wholesale distribution is a different mindset and cost structure. For the "farm to fork" supply chain, using a third party shipper that isn't in the food business might be the more compelling alternative. The farmer who uses a much bigger food industry player to bring the harvest to market will risk losing control over whom he or she sells to, and at what price. Moreover, having your sustainably produced harvest or value-added product delivered by a truck branded with the name of a national distributor of conventionally grown and overly processed food is going to taint the experience for the buyer and diminish the trust that only exists in locally executed transactions (thus the aforementioned practice of national distributors creating separate subsidiaries to go after the local opportunity).

Callicrate, the lead plaintiff in a now longstanding lawsuit against the world's largest meat packer for discriminatory practices, is less politic. Those local subsidiaries of the national distributors are "attempts at putting window dressing...on a wholesale sector that takes too much and blocks access" to markets, via predatory pricing, prohibitively high insurance and minimum order requirements, expensive third-party verification, and other more nefarious activities. The more direct the better for a new local food system. The goal, he says, is to keep increasing the farm share of the consumer retail dollar.

Traditional wholesale distributors will have their place. In particular, restaurants that weren't initially structured (like Inovasi) to work directly with farmers but still want to source locally made produce will want their distributor to carry sustainable food options. The same probably goes for national grocery store chains. Small neighborhood markets and food cooperatives, however, are already buying directly from growers.

There is a new kind of wholesale distributor coming to Chicago that, like Inovasi, is structuring itself from the beginning to better service local restaurants with food produced in the region. Dave Rand and Andrew Lutsey have formed a new company, Chicago Local Food, for just that purpose. Together they bring a unique combination of skills well suited for the task. To help create Chicago Local Food, Lutsey is leaving the 600-acre family farm in Wisconsin where he ran everything from sales and marketing to the presence at farmer's markets. Situated near Green Bay, Lutsey is intimately familiar with the logistical challenges of getting a farm's products to a large market several hours away. Rand, for his part, has worked more off the farm that on it, including a two-year stint at the Green City Market in downtown Chicago. Together, they know all the farmers in the region, and know the problems they have servicing the restaurants in the city profitably. Enter Chicago Local Food. The company will first and foremost act as a regional food hub right in Chicago, with its own distribution center and fleet of delivery trucks. That won't help the farmer in Urbana, however, so the company is building its network of "aggregators," or food hubs in a region that extends 350 miles from the city. If there is a hole in the network (as there is in central and southern Illinois), Chicago Local Food will build the food hub itself. The major differences between this regional food hub and a national distribution system are that Chicago Local Food will be representing farmers from towns you, the consumer, have heard of or even visited. You may even have tried that farm's offerings at a farmers market. Smaller isn't just "beautiful" (as author E.F. Schumacher wrote); smaller makes any business or service easier to analyze for quality and credibility. Notice also that this already small local distribution capability (and opportunity) is further subdivided between two different services (i.e., Chicago Local Foods servicing restaurants and grocery, and Irv and Shelly's handling direct-to-home delivery).

These hubs existed a long time ago. They were sometimes called regional packing sheds. But when the retail food industry consolidated, the network disappeared. That process eliminated an important market for small farmers. Chicago Local Food wants to rebuild that network in the Midwest. In its simplest form, the new aggregation point will have a refrigerated warehouse. Some will add a commercial kitchen with processing capability. In the company's vision, all of them will be connected through a network of third party logistics companies and less-than-truckload carriers. The partners are raising millions of dollars to make it all happen.

If Chicago Local Food is successful, it will look just as Irv Cernauskas and Chef des Rosier envisioned, and possibly possess elements of the shared community kitchen that Ron and his wife need, and Alexis and Zina have sought to provide. Musing the absurdity of the current supply chain more than anything, Irv suggests that for the city of Chicago, it is currently easier to source from China than it is Urbana, Illinois. The existing supply chain is oriented towards a global food system and doesn't serve the local market very well. As a consequence, a state like Illinois, blessed from birth with among the most fertile soils in the world, imports 90% of what the residents eat from outside of state (while exporting dollars), and exports at least that much of what we grow.

Environmentally, nutritionally, and economically, it doesn't make sense to ship long distances food that can be produced locally. Echoing Mike Callicrate, Cernauskas sees that a flat distribution system will serve the farmer and retail customer best. Independent, less-than-truckload carriers are the best partners in that endeavor, so you don't end up "the mouse against the elephant." Restaurants, in my opinion, will need something more at the other end of the spectrum. Thus the need for Chicago Local Food. The development of food hubs and transportation services is a natural step in the evolution of the local food network. A grower doesn't easily go from selling at farmers market directly to selling to food wholesalers, even if that were the goal.

# CHAPTER 13

## Soil

"The soil is the great connector of lives, the source and destination of all. It is the healer and restorer and resurrector, by which disease passes into health, age into youth, death into life. Without proper care for it we can have no community, because without proper care for it we can have no life." – Wendell Berry, *The Unsettling of America: Culture and Agriculture*

I met up with Erlene Howard of Collective Resource at the Brothers K Coffee House in Evanston. It was 9 o'clock on a Friday morning, and I had to wait for someone to leave to get a seat. This was great to see, half a block down from a Starbucks.

Erlene looks the part of business executive: together, mature, and thoughtful. You would not guess that she was running a start-up composting operation. Collective Resource is just that. With a single Dodge Sprinter, a few assistants, and a line of credit, Elrene is collecting and distributing food waste from over a hundred individuals and 25 restaurants, all of whom pay her to take it away. It wasn't always this cushy.

She started in 2008, making pickups and deliveries in her Toyota Camry, just as I'd started doing with my Toyota Highlander. After a career as a bookkeeper, Erlene wasn't leveraging that experience into a related career, or taking two steps to the right before marching forward in to the white-collar world. She had completely broken from the past and had done it, like so many people in this story, in mid-life. With little more than a personal interest in organic and simple food, Erlene took the advice of a friend who told her to "just start doing it."

Initially Erlene modeled the business after the company Earth Girl Composting in Vermont. Founded by Megan Kolbay in 2006, Earth Girl Composting provides five gallon buckets to customers and transports the contents to a local composting facility or farm on a weekly or monthly basis. Then Erlene met Ken Dunn, a superhero within Chicago's sustainable living community, who taught her the basics of what she needed to know to get going. It took Collective Resource 6 months to haul the first ton and two years to haul 100 tons. Individual customers pay her to take food waste away, because they know it's a good idea. Her customers have shirts at the dry cleaner, a cleaning service for dusting the house, and would love to compost, but don't have the time. Enter Collective Resource.

For a little over $10, Collective Resource picks up a 5-gallon bucket of food waste, and leaves an empty bucket in its place. The restaurants also pay Collective Resource, but they would be paying for all their waste removal anyway. For some restaurants, it is simply an economic decision, and Erlene must compete with the landfill. Until she has the land to compost herself, and until a technology she likes is available, Erlene has the food waste brought to a commercial composting facility, usually owned by the local waste hauler. (At a commercial composting facility, she can compost anything that was once alive, including meat scraps and paper plates, because of the high heat level generated by the larger mounds of compost). Ken Dunn's model is very different. It is a closed loop, Chicago's loop, from food waste to food and back again.

Ken Dunn has scars older than most of the participants in the sustainable food movement. He's also stronger, faster, and smarter, according to those who know him best.[30] After a stint in the Peace Corps and post-graduate studies in philosophy, in 1972, Dunn founded the Resource Center. Forty years later, the non-profit has an annual budget in the millions, and operations spanning recycling, composting, farming, and bicycle repair. But it's the composting and farming loop that is of most interest here. For decades, the Resource Center has been taking in food waste, composting that food waste, and returning it to the soil on one of the Dunn's "farms." There, Dunn and his team of 30 full-time people, plus around 100 part-time volunteers, grow a prodigious quantity of vegetables, including a lot of peppers, for some of the best restaurants in Chicago.

Neither Dunn nor the Resource Center owns any of this urban farmland. The Resource Center is granted use of the land by the city of Chicago until that particular lot is chosen for commercial development. Then, the city grants Dunn access to a different lot, and the Resource Center moves on. There are 20,000 such lots around the city. With such favorable access to land, it's conceivable that the farming portion of the Resource Center could be profitable on its own. But Dunn's other ambitions, like social equality, justice, and education, have been served best by his commitment to the non-profit model.

Right now, Erlene's "business" is dependent on the desire of customers to live a more sustainable lifestyle at their own expense. Not necessarily so for Ken Dunn; his commercial customers have to pay fees more directly tied to volume (relative to a residential customer of Erlene's) to have this "waste" taken away. In both markets, composting food waste is more than environmentally conscious waste management for society as a whole. Composting is the process, especially in the absence of livestock, by which nutrients are returned to the soil that gives us back our food. Look down the side of a one-a-day multivitamin bottle (or the side of a cereal box). The minerals, or micronutrients, listed there are all critical to human health (and for that matter, plant and animal health). No matter how small the quantity necessary, we won't be healthy without those traces of copper, manganese, and zinc. Before they came from a bottle, we got these micronutrients from our food. Our food, animal or vegetable, would directly or indirectly get those nutrients from the soil. Over 50 years ago, Andre Voisin wrote, "The organism (animal or human) is the 'biochemical photograph' of the environment in which it lives, particularly of the soil which manufactures nutrients for it."

According to the EPA, 36 million tons of food waste was generated in 2011, with all but 4% of it winding up in landfill. What if we were successful in reducing our food waste to zero? What if the composting industry lost its main feedstock? Adding nitrogen, phosphorous, and potassium alone will make plants grow, but not plants that will produce healthy humans. How would we return fertility and nutrients to the soil in the absence of such a composting program? Although this scenario might be pure fantasy, thinking about it is instructive; you would suddenly find that having livestock as part of a diverse farming operation was necessary for more than just making sausage. When a former seminary prospect writes a book in praise of manure and calls it *Holy Shit*, it pays to listen. Says Gene Logsdon, "...those people within our society who seem bent on getting rid of the livestock industry would be thrown into a quandary. They might start to look upon husbandry with a little more kindness if they understood that without it, they might not be able to grow enough fruits and vegetables for everyone."[31] His passion for poop is not based on a leap of faith. This is a detailed account of how what goes in one end directly affects what comes out the other. Even the art of matching bedding (flax, straw, wood chips, sawdust) with buffalo chips gets the coverage it deserves in his book. The rapid increase in the demand for manure (a sign both of the movement towards sustainability and the unsustainable costs of artificial fertilizer) is so great, claims Logsdon, there is a farmer in his neck of the woods who is keeping cows just for the waste stream. That's no bull.

Are the concepts of composting and soil "fertility" really that important? Or is it all just so much tree hugging. If there is a modern godfather of sustainable and organic agriculture, it is Sir Albert Howard. What Howard thought of as "organic" is more akin to what we now call "sustainable" agriculture generally, and polyculture (multiple species of plants and animals on the same farm) specifically. In Howard's world, the sustainable farmer doesn't grow *vegetables* so much as he or she does *soil*.

Sir Albert Howard's simple premise, that a disease in one of his crops meant that *he*, as a farmer, was doing something wrong, is easily applied to analysis of the human condition. Poor health is not the normal state of man. If I'm sick, I'm likely not taking proper care of myself. The response should be, as it was for Howard, to find out the root cause of the issue your body is directing you to. Howard's biographer and second wife, Louise, summarized her husband's view of the connection between soil and health this way:

> "A fertile soil, that is, a soil teeming with healthy life in the shape of abundant microflora and microfauna, will bear healthy plants, and these, when consumed by animals and man, will confer health on animals and man. But an infertile soil, that is, one lacking sufficient microbial fungous, and other life, will pass on some form of deficiency to the plant, and such plant, in turn, will pass on some form of deficiency to animal and man."[32]

Good health, said Sir Albert, is the birthright of all living things, including crops and humans. *Health* is the natural state. Disease along the chain is a marker; something in the agricultural system is off plumb. Undernourishment of the soil, found Howard, is the root of it all. The soil is the 'creative material' of most of the basic needs of life, wrote Dr. William Albrecht in concurrence. All creation starts with a handful of dust.

# PART IV

# Business Hurdles

# CHAPTER 14

# Greenwashing

"Advertising is the art of convincing people to spend money they don't have on something they don't need."
– Will Rogers

"Greenwash – verb: the act of misleading consumers regarding the environmental practices of a company or the environmental benefits of a product or service." – Underwriters Laboratory

Eating food that has been sustainably brought forth is the single best thing you can do for human and environmental health. At point of purchase, local and organic food costs more than conventionally grown food. As a consequence, there are food producers that will attempt to get consumers to pay that local and organic premium for a product that is something less than advertised, scoring some extra profit with little real effort. That attempt to fool you is the sustainable food movement's version of environmental greenwashing.

But the market for local products has a built in defense mechanism, a greenwash repellent, if you will. You can import and export just about anything, including organic food, but you can't import and export "local."

## The Local Solution

Consequently, false advertising in the market for local, whole foods (minimally-processed vegetables, meat, and dairy) is going to be more difficult than in the market for packaged goods. The firefight will be over the use and meaning of the word "local." Is local within 100 miles or 250 miles? I don't know that it matters as much at this level of granularity unless the products are identical in quality. If the pork pastured in Iowa is better than the pork pastured in Illinois, the Chicago restaurants are going to use the pork from Iowa. It's up to the farmers in Illinois to figure out how to make their product at least as good as what the buyer can get by driving a little further on down the road. For the consumer, at least, it's not more complicated than asking, "so, where's your farm?" No need to run to the USDA website to parse words, at least not yet. I'm hopeful that there will be no need for a federal referee or third party verifier. I think we are safe for now, until such time that there is big money in a little thing called the local food movement.

### History of Greenwashing

When the practice of trying to get environmentally conscious consumers to pay a premium for products that were less friendly to the earth than advertised, the environmental community gave it a name: greenwashing. It implies whitewashing with illusory environmental ("green") attributes. Whatever analogy you want to use, the practice of greenwashing, and the act of exposing it, frustrates well-meaning producers and makes customers cynical. This combination can be poisonous to market growth, especially after a customer discovers he or she has been burned (i.e., suckered into paying a premium price for a product without the perceived benefits). Thus, it's relevant to the business of increasing demand for sustainable food.

The practice of what became known as greenwashing in environmental circles started at the crossroads of health and nutrition. The concept today is straightforward. To use the market for environmentally friendly products as an example, as consumers increasingly demonstrate the willingness to pay a premium for products that do less damage to the environment, consumer products companies have devised ways to frame their products in just the right light to make the products look environmentally friendly, or "green." Sometimes the technique is as subtle as using colors on packaging to conjure up images of nature, or even literal representations of the same (pictures of trees, leaves, mountains, lakes). Sometimes the slight of hand is designed to get you the consumer to focus on one attribute so that you will ignore another, less flattering product trait.

If you have a sense of humor, some of the more shameless efforts are entertaining. For example, oil companies touting modest investments in alternative energy, or flowers sprouting from a chimney.[33] Other greenwashing programs are more elaborate, such as the ones claiming to be backed by "science." Greenwashing claims are often backed by no science, bad science, or third-party research funded by the polluters.

In the United States, ethanol derived from corn as a green alternative to gasoline is an entire *industry* based on greenwashing, and it's had a huge, negative impact on agriculture. The ethanol market is that rare example of government and industry working harmoniously together (tongue firmly in beak). Ethanol was supposed to fix everything that ails us, from global warming to high gas prices and dependence on foreign oil. That was the theory, at least. U.S. car manufacturers have been more than happy to be complicit in the scheme. Instead of investing in hybrid electric technology, the U.S. manufacturers trumpeted "flex fuel" capabilities, which allowed the car to run either on gasoline or 85% ethanol. Flex fuel required no investment by the manufacturers, because so many of their vehicles could already run on the higher blend without any changes. Advertisements with green and yellow pictures of corn were splashed across every major periodical as a way to promote the environmental benefits of ethanol. Since leaving the political arena, even Al Gore, once a champion of ethanol, has admitted the error of his ways. But that horse left the gate years ago. Now, 40% of the corn crop in the U.S., some 35 million acres of farmland, is dedicated to producing a fuel that is no more environmentally friendly than oil, but 30% less efficient (your car would not drive as far on a gallon of ethanol compared to a gallon of gasoline). Further factor in the contribution to rising food costs from allocating so much farmland to corn destined for an ethanol plant, the net effect of this nation's corn-based ethanol program is almost certainly negative, not the great energy or environmental solution it was promised to be. Author Barbara Tuchman argues that to qualify as "folly," a policy must meet three criteria. First, it must been known to be counter-productive in its time. Second, a feasible alternative must have been available. Third, a group, not a single dominant personality, should have made the policy in question.[34] If our ethanol program doesn't qualify as folly, I don't know what does.

## Sustainable Food Greenwashing

Organic. 100% Organic. All Natural. Natural. Fair Trade. Grass Fed. Grain Fed. Grass Finished. Certified Humane. Non-GMO Certified. Antibiotic Free. Hormone Free. Free Range. Cage Free. Guilt Free.

Okay, I made that last one up. (I personally haven't seen it on a food label; that doesn't mean someone hasn't tried to use it somewhere). But the rest are all claims made on food labels designed to separate the consumer from his or her money. Some claims are accurate and helpful; other claims are nothing more than a deceptive practice designed so the manufacturer can get something (a premium price) for nothing. Snake oil salesmen are alive and well in the 21st century.

Not surprisingly perhaps, given the organic food movement's roots in environmentalism, greenwashing has invaded the grocery store shelves. The sustainable food movement needs its own word for deceptive and confusing claims that undermines the industry. I've heard the term "food fraud" used and think it has great potential. Since this book began with a discussion about eggs, this seems to be a good place to begin the discussion of "food fraud."

In talking to legislators, farmers, and backyard chicken advocates, I have made two points repeatedly in defense of backyard chicken coops. The first is that the product you get from your backyard hens cannot be purchased in the grocery store. The second is that trying to sell organic eggs from pastured hens off the farm (i.e., through distribution) is an exceedingly difficult, and in some geographies impossible, business in which to make enough money to justify the investment.

Let's start with the most common label claim aimed at getting the consumer to pay a higher price for eggs: "cage-free." This label is obviously in response to growing distaste for the factory farm model in general, and specifically the system of putting laying hens in cages too small to even allow the bird to flap its wings for exercise. The bird lives like this for its entire productive life. Now, imagine you have a hundred thousand hens in wall-to-wall small cages in a single warehouse; remove the cages, but keep the hens wing-to-wing in the same crowded warehouse. Technically the bird is "cage-free," but it still lives in conditions that are not conducive to good health for the bird or the consumer. The USDA does not recognize the term "cage-free," nor is it verifiable by any third party. Therefore, the claim doesn't really have any value by itself. Of course, if you have the chance to visit the farm and verify the claim for yourself, that's another story. Know your farmer whenever possible.

The next label claim designed to justify a higher retail price is "free-range." According to the USDA, the term is applied to poultry (and only poultry as of this writing) when said poultry has "access" to the outside. The quality and quantity of that space is not specified. Consumers might understandably see the term "free-range" and assume that the chickens get to spend the majority of their days on grass or pasture. This may in fact be true for certain brands, or it may not. As with the cage-free label, the free-range claim might mean that the hens spend most of the day in the same cramped conditions of the warehouse used to cage hens, but the cages are removed. If there is a small door in the corner of the warehouse leading to a cement patio, technically the eggs and broilers can be labeled free-range. The hens can therefore move around the warehouse but are still unlikely to have access to greener pastures. One of the negative consequences of this living situation is debeaking, in which farmers cut the birds' beaks off to minimize the damage done by the chickens attacking each other due to the duress of crowded conditions. Also, without meaningful access to green pasture, there is no nutritional benefit worth paying for in this version of "free-range" as it relates to poultry products.

This is not to say that the USDA doesn't have rules governing word choice on labels for products and nutrition claims. The USDA defines Eggs Benedict (must contain 18 percent cured smoked ham, a poached egg on a toasted English muffin, and be covered in hollandaise sauce), Egg Foo Young with poultry (must contain 3% poultry), and "fresh" eggs. For an egg to be anointed as fresh has nothing to do with the time passed since it was laid, or the distance from farm to fork. It must be in the shell or broken, but not dry or frozen. Thank goodness! Though defined by the USDA, the standard for "free-range" is pretty useless bordering on deceptive for consumers willing to pay a premium for poultry products enhanced by daily access to green acres during the life of the bird.

Some labels are accurate in identifying the way the product is produced but still play upon a misperception in the market place as to the value of the particular claim. For instance, there is a fair bit of emphasis placed on feeding hens a 100% vegetarian diet. This is interesting because as we know, a hen is an omnivore – allowed to live on pasture or your backyard, they will eat worms and insects. The vegetarian diet for chickens, like the vegetarian and vegan movements, is a commendable reaction to the reality that chickens were being fed animal byproducts, specifically parts of other chickens. Forced cannibalism. The same was done with beef cattle, and that didn't work out so well (the practice is believed to have contributed to the evolution of bovine spongiform encephalopathy, or Mad Cow Disease).

At least you can rest assured that if you buy a product that is Certified Organic according to USDA standards, the product is in fact totally organic, right? Well, no. As it turns out, Certified Organic is only 95% organic. How one can calculate how much in the way of chemical influences are allowed before breaching the 95% threshold is beyond me. I'm guessing it is beyond the comprehension of a lot of farmers and consumers, too. Nevertheless, it leaves the door open for yet another label claim to make its way to the grocery shelf in the recent past: "100% Organic." Of course, as already mentioned, the USDA standards for organic certification (according to the National Organic Program, or NOP) now allow over 70 inorganic chemicals to be used in the process.

I am desperate not to sound cynical about organic certification. Before the standards existed, deceptive or misleading practices hurt the market for sustainable food and screamed for some kind of regulation. But as we've seen, regulation hasn't necessarily solved all the problems. Some organic farmers and food producers resent the government take-over of organic certification and the third party verification industry the act spawned. But at least, whether any individual agrees with the standards or not, you pretty much know what the term "certified organic" means. To adapt Winston Churchill's comments about democracy to fit this discussion, our current system of organic certification may be the worst system imaginable, except for the all the others yet tried.

The obvious way to address this problem is to know your farmer. Character, as the saying goes, is what you do when no one is looking. Many farmers would do the right thing without regulation, and may even go further than the regulations require. But you can't know which ones have character and are raising food with respect for the environment and the plants and animals they're cultivating until you get to know the farmers. How do you make sure that your omnivorous egg laying Rhode Island Red is getting a species-appropriate diet but isn't eating the remains of other dead chickens? Make sure that Red is spending her days on grass, eating whatever bugs and worms might make themselves available. If you can't drive to a farm and witness it yourself, it's time to start your own backyard flock.

I opted out of the egg market by making backyard hens a part of my lifestyle. I largely opted out of the mass produced organic vegetable supply chain, with its roots in California (technically organic, but not sustainable), by joining a CSA farm in my county. Now I've added grass-fed beef, pork, and chicken to the rotation, but here again greenwashing is a problem. Given the price premium for grass-fed beef (over corn-fed beef), no one should be shocked that suppliers are trying to cash in on the growing demand. The USDA passed a grass-fed standard back in 2007 that embraced pasture grazing in both spirit and practice. The standard states "grass and/or forage shall be the feed source consumed for the lifetime of the ruminant animal, with the exception of milk consumed prior to weaning. The diet shall be derived solely from forage and the animals cannot be fed grain or grain by-products and must have continuous access to pasture during the growing season."

But I regularly see advertisements for grass-fed beef in restaurants that upon review are not produced in accordance with the USDA standard. Specifically, the cattle are fed corn for the majority of their lives, and only "finished" on grass. This does, according to one study out of Cornell University, have the benefit of diminishing the growth of acidic *e. coli* strains in the cows' stomach that would be dangerous to humans. The nutritional content of the beef, however, is still a function of the diet over the lifetime of the animal. If you want the benefits of grass-fed beef and are willing to pay for it, you really need to ask if the meat is from a 100% grass-fed animal.

One of the more devious and depressing developments in the market for grass-fed beef has taken place in the world of bison, or buffalo, meat. In a restaurant that wants to offer a "healthy" alternative to hamburgers from corn-fed cattle, it is increasingly common to see "buffalo burgers" on the menu. The description of the item will be replete with all the health benefits of eating buffalo meat over industrial beef: it's leaner, lower in fat and calories, yet higher in protein. Of course, the health benefits of buffalo meat historically have had less to do with the animal species itself, and more to do with the fact that the buffalo were grazed continuously on pasture (i.e., 100% grass fed). As in prior examples, unscrupulous producers looking to get something for nothing started putting buffalo in stalls, feeding them corn, and charging a grass-fed premium for the end result.

Author and rancher (Wild Idea Buffalo Company) Dan O'Brien describes the adoption of the cattle-industry model by buffalo ranchers best: "...feed the buffalo grain in what amounts to a feedlot and deal with the diseases associated with non-natural feeding by use of vaccinations and antibiotics. It's a little like locking children in a room with ice cream and potato chips and treating the health problems that result with expensive medicine."[35] No one knows for sure, but it's possible that as many as 90% of bison in the U.S. spend at least the last two months before slaughter in a feed lot. Mr. O'Brien looked out the window of his home as we spoke. He could see his bison heard, three miles away, for the first time in a month. The animals have over 20,000 acres of grasslands to roam. The bison evolved over millions of years to live in harmony with the grass on this flat but rugged landscape. They don't require moveable fences or someone to tell them when they should move on before doing damage to the land. The bison do it instinctively, and produce prodigious amounts of healthy meat in the process. All it takes is time. More time, unfortunately, than some folks think is worth waiting.

The customer orders a buffalo burger thinking he or she is avoiding the negative consequences of corn-fed beef. Too often the customer is being deceived at best and simply ripped off at worst. Even some farm-raised fish are now being fed corn. There seems to be no limit to the ways corn is being used to cheapen both the quality and the price of food. Know your rancher!

# CHAPTER 15

# Price versus Value

"Price is what you pay. Value is what you get." –Warren Buffet

Here is a pet peeve. If I told you that I that I would sell you my Rolex watch, worth $5,000, for only $500, your shyster radar would go off. You would likely walk away. You would know, instinctively, that either the watch was a fake, or that it was stolen. Either way, you wouldn't reach for your wallet. But tell the average American that they can get a meal for a dollar, and they line up down the street and around the corner. Where is that healthy skepticism when it comes to offers of low-priced food?

Yes, people can live without watches; they can't live without food. Yet we each spend (I hope) a whole lot more on food every day, week, month, and year, then we spend on watches, and we buy food with much greater frequency. Not every American has the purchasing power to be choosy in the grocery store. But too few of those that can are applying anything like critical thinking when making food purchases. Everybody likes getting a bargain. Some of the wealthiest people I know are also the thriftiest. But what is a "bargain" when it comes to food? If you venture out from backyard farmsteading into budding food entrepreneur, you can expect to be faced with this and related questions about price versus value when it comes to food.

I like the word "value" in this discussion about the price we pay to eat. It's a relative world, and nothing exemplifies that quite like the concept of value. Too often the discussions about what value means devolve into something related only to price. I am spending $25 on meat, but how much meat am I getting in return? If something is cheaper, it must be a better value. But is it?

Related to the previously mentioned topic of greenwashing, this chapter is about the broad swath of American consumers battling misinformation, taking the time to understand the value of good food, and starting to pay attention to what they get, or don't get, with each food dollar.

Whether food or watches or sneakers or cars, a big chunk of the world seems to think that cheaper is always better. Lots of very intelligent people still don't see any benefit to paying a premium for local or organic food. It's difficult to convince most people, especially someone living paycheck to paycheck, that benefits received a decade down the road are worth paying a premium for today (even when those benefits are related to physical health). Few consumers, especially those without extra disposable income, want to hear about the "externalized costs" of the industrial food system. That is understandable. We are all busy and many of us are "just getting by." This is an unavoidable reality for aspiring providers in the sustainable food movement.

Fortunately for me, my customers, and the "early adopters" you come across in the sustainable food movement today, generally fall into another category. Though as I've said before, there is no "one" average consumer either in the sustainable food movement or at Backyard Chicken Run, there are a few common threads behind the decision to "go sustainable." Even though society isn't (yet) internalizing the social cost of an unsustainable form of agriculture, some of my customers make that calculation themselves for personal reasons. Most feel strongly about the need to source their food more closely to home (the major theme in this book). Others might be doing it for personal health concerns. Others just don't want to contribute to "those big company" participants in industrial food production. Few of my customers would be considered rich, and I'm guessing most of them choose not to buy some other consumer good so they can afford to eat sustainably. They are fortunate to be able to make that choice. However they've managed to pull it off, these customers, when they can, spend their money in a way that is consistent with their *personal* values. That's the real reason I like the word "value" in this discussion, even more so than "worth."

The next wave of "good food" consumers are by definition *not* early adopters. What follows, then, is an exercise in looking at the things we spend money on that overlap someway with food. What follows is an attempt to shift the discussion about whether good (organic and local) food is both worth the higher initial price, and affordable to the average American.

## Compared to What?

We Americans spend less on food as a percentage of our income than at any point in our history, and less as a percentage of our income than people from other developed countries. But we spend a lot of money on other stuff we might not need to buy if we spent more on good food. It was during my first job out of college that I met a wonderful executive assistant. One day she was walking past my desk after lunch and caught me popping a handful of vitamins into my mouth. "You know, John, if you ate properly, you wouldn't need to take those." Amen. Americans are spending over $20 billion a year on nutritional supplements. That's about the size of the market for organic foods just a few years ago. This is not a criticism of the supplement industry; mineral deficiency is likely a major contributor to chronic disease, and plants can't manufacture their own minerals. If the minerals aren't in the soil, they aren't in the plant. That's one of the first things to understand when it comes to evaluating the cost-benefit proposition of paying more for sustainably grown food. Food produced in conventionally cultivated, mineral-deficient soil *must* be less nutritious than food produced in soil that has the full complement of minerals replenish between growing seasons through the application of organic matter. Once last year's crop draws out the minerals in the soil, those minerals, other than just nitrogen, phosphorous, and potassium, need to somehow be replaced. Sustainable agriculture does that. Conventional agriculture doesn't. I'm also not talking about nutrient deficiency caused by choosing kettle corn over kale. I'm talking specifically about the nutritional superiority of grass-fed beef over conventional corn-fed beef, and the nutritional superiority of the tomato grown locally in organic soil versus the tomato grown in sand a thousand miles away and consumed weeks after harvest (vegetables starting losing taste and nutritional content soon after getting picked).

Over thirty billion dollars is spent annually in the "alternative medicine" category, which overlaps with the nutritional supplement market. Says Marion Nestle, "the preponderance of available evidence suggests that if they were tested, the great majority of supplements now on the market would prove no more effective than placebos and that a few would be demonstrably harmful."[36] Dr. Robert Lustig estimates the market for "nutraceuticals," or nutritional supplements, genetically engineered foods, and processed foods that reportedly have health benefits, at $100 billion. When it comes to the intersection of diabetes and cardiovascular disease, diet (more vegetables and fruit at the expense of sugar and processed foods) is "almost uniformly beneficial in improving the signs and symptoms of metabolic syndrome."[37] Supplements, it would appear aren't doing the job alone. So we remain overweight, out of shape, and unhealthy. What do we do? We spend another $25 billion on memberships to health and fitness clubs. Together, the few categories above represent somewhere north of $125 billion, outside of healthcare, that we spend to offset the negative consequences of "cheap" food. It looks less and less like a value to me.

## Healthcare

Ten years ago, I received the first test results saying that my cholesterol and triglycerides were too high. This was before becoming more informed about the impact of diet on health. I attempted to remedy the problem by shifting the emphasis of my daily exercise from lifting weights to sweating. I shared the change in philosophy with a couple of guys who I saw at the gym every morning. They looked at me like I had six heads. "Just go on Lipitor…Doesn't cost anything," one of them said to me. *It doesn't cost anything.* Wow. The words have ricocheted off the inside of my skull for a decade. Every time I hear about the skyrocketing cost of healthcare I think of that morning. I also think of that conversation every time someone says that good food is unaffordable.

If you don't see any cost to healthcare, then this particular debate is going to fall on deaf ears. I happen to have what is known as a health savings account, or a health plan with a very high deductible. I get to save what I don't spend of my deductible in an investment account that compounds tax free, like an individual retirement account, or IRA. If I spend money on cholesterol or blood pressure medication, that's *my* money. This *costs* me something. The money I'm *not* spending on pharmaceuticals is my money, too. I can't help but think that if everyone who either bought health insurance or had health insurance provided to them had a high deductible health savings account, the good food movement would get a boost, and the total expenditure on healthcare would go down. We spend over $2 trillion a year on health care, twice what we spend on food. That relationship was flipped a generation ago. Americans spend over a billion dollars just on antacids. We spent $260 billion at retail on prescription drugs in 2010. Thirty billion of that was just for the class of drugs known as statins, prescribed to lower cholesterol with the goal of preventing heart disease. The business opportunity, through education (and more education) is to take back market share (or what marketers refer to as "share of wallet") from the pharmaceutical and nutritional supplement industries. Organic farmers need to start selling nutrition, not just taste and chemical avoidance.

### Portion Size

Let's assume you know the differences between labels and that you've had a chance to talk to the farmers who have produced the food available to you. You can also identify the steak that came from a factory farm a thousand miles away versus the one raised on nearby pasture. As you reach for your wallet, you notice the price for the 8 ounces of grass-fed filet is higher than the same sized corn-fed steak. Is the premium price worth it?

I am now going to ask you to take a small leap of faith. Most of the literature analyzing nutrition, hunger, overeating, and obesity, focuses on glucose swings. But obviously even people that avoid sugar feel pangs of hunger. Other than the need for energy (calories), that feeling of hunger is a function of your body's need for nutrients. In the animal world generally, and among pregnant women specifically, the dynamic is known as "pica" or "cribbing." Overweight people and binge eaters have the same cravings, but those cravings unfortunately manifest themselves in the form of fried, processed, and sugary foods.[38] And those foods are habit forming. It's a brutal cycle. But there is a way to break it.

Everyone I know who has made the switch to a whole food sustainable diet has said the same thing: Eating organic produce and pastured proteins regularly satiates hunger more quickly (i.e., after eating a smaller quantity of food) than when eating grains, processed food, and corn-fed beef. I personally believe that it is the superior nutritional content of the whole food sustainable diet. For example, I am "full" from eating an 8-ounce grass-fed steak. Before my conversion to sustainable eating it might have taken me a 10 or 12 ounces of corn-fed beef to feel as full. It makes sense to me. As Dr. Lustig says in *Fat Chance*, a calorie is not a calorie. Ever hear someone say they feel "iron deficient?" I have felt that way. That's when I crave red meat, and eating red meat makes the craving go away. I feel like either my brain tells my stomach or my stomach tells my brain when I am in need of something, either energy or nutrition, and I feel hungry. Your stomach has its own brain, the Enteric Nervous System, or ENS. In evolutionary terms, the ENS came before the Central Nervous System, and the latter left the former intact and capable of making some of its own decisions. Consequently, as an infant, we eat before we can think. As adults, we just eat without thinking.

It probably doesn't hurt that I chew better tasting food longer. That makes sense, too. What do you do when you take awful tasting medicine? You swallow it as quickly as possible. It's the same with food that either tastes bad or just lacks taste in general. But when that steak is rich and flavorful, and causes you to moan involuntarily, you chew it longer. This allows for more digestion to get started while the food is in the mouth, and more full digestion and nutrient absorption, throughout the entire gastrointestinal tract. More nutrition enters the blood stream, and your body (and your brain) can *taste* that.

Says Dr. Lustig, "The simple act of food processing removes the food's native micronutrients, just as the fiber is stripped away. After all, micronutrients travel with the fiber." It's worth repeating that the majority of the elements of food processing and the negative consequences it brings are implemented primarily to extend shelf life and prepare food for travel over long distances. Excessive use of sugar and salt is a reaction to the loss of taste in processed, shelf stable food. Moreover, vegetables start losing nutritional content soon after they are picked. The anecdote (if it isn't already obvious) is to buy fresh, local food in its whole form. To finish with the beef, if a 10-ounce grass-fed steak fills you up as well as a 12-ounce corn-fed steak, a 20% premium in price for the former is really no premium at all. In the discussion of value versus cost, then, I argue that local produce and pastured proteins, though more "expensive" upfront per portion, end up being no more expensive because you end up needing to eat less to be sated.

# CHAPTER 16

# GMO (Give Me Organic)

"...the single most serious strategic threat to the global food system is the threat of genetic erosion: the loss of germplasm and the increased vulnerability of food crops to their natural enemies." – Al Gore

The market "opportunity" produced by the proliferation of genetically modified food for the sustainable food entrepreneur is huge. Even in the absence of a labeling law that requires the disclosure of genetically modified elements in a food product, if consumers ever decide en masse that buying non-gmo food is important to them, the organic food movement is set to explode. How that decision gets made is the "local" opportunity. The opportunity is in communication between providers and consumers. Most consumers don't have a degree in biology, and they trust their farmers a lot more than their politicians or scientists at big agribusiness companies. I don't know that all genetically engineered food products are necessarily bad. I feel comfortable saying that not all genetically engineered food products come without risk.

How is the consumer supposed to digest all of this? This is a timely question because of the recent (as of this writing) referendum in California that would have required food products containing genetically modified organisms to be labeled as such. A labeling requirement seemed like a reasonable and low cost way to inform consumers about what they were eating. It didn't pass. I lost no sleep. The reality is that as a consumer, if you buy any product containing a grain for which there is a genetically modified alternative on the market (or if your are consuming meat or dairy that isn't organic), you can assume with a high degree of certainty that you are consuming GMOs. No label necessary. If you don't like that idea, than buy organic. Certified organic standards forbid the use of genetically engineered ingredients. It's not a panacea; GMOs are verboten by the government's National Organic Program, but not tested (thus the emergence of yet another third party verification option, "certified non-GMO"). Still, the option is yours. Together, farmers and local consumers can separate the wheat from the chaff, and move global agriculture from triage to sustainability.

## Background

Around 280 BC, King Pyrrhus of Epirus took his army into battle at Asculum against the Romans. Just as he had done in Heraclea, Pyrrhus crushed the opposing army, inflicting disproportionate casualties upon the enemy. It came, however, at a great cost. So many of his friends and field commanders were killed in the battle, an exasperated Pyrrhus declared that another such "victory" and the Greeks would be ruined.

I can't help but think of this story when I think about the proliferation of industrial and technological solutions to problems that are implemented without adequate consideration for external costs. Al Gore, for his part, thought genetically engineering crops was more akin to doing a deal with the devil. We are still haunted, he mused, by "Faustian bargains made when older technologies were introduced, many of them much less sophisticated than modern genetic engineering."[39] And that was back in 1992. Today, all I can do, all any consumer can do, is to try and understand what GMOs are and why they are causing such concern. Through this exercise, I began to understand why most sustainable eaters think that banning GMOs is one of the things that "certified organic" got right.

## What Are They?

Genetically engineered (GE) crops, or genetically modified organisms as they are commonly called, generally come in one of three flavors.

The seeds are being genetically engineered for nutritional fortification, pest resistance, or pesticide resistance. The last two factors attract the most negative attention, but I'll start with nutritional fortification.

Through the years we have fortified food staples such as flour with riboflavin to prevent rickets, thiamin to prevent beriberi, iron to prevent anemia, and niacin, or Vitamin B, to prevent pellagra. Milk is fortified with vitamin D and salt with iodine. Some eggs are now fortified with Omega-3's. Though some fortification is done for marketing purposes, the practice really has its roots in the treatment of disease.

Staples like flour have been enriched since the forties, as William Alexander points out in his book *52 Loaves*. Intended to be a book about bread and life, it also offers a thoughtful introduction to the field of nutritional deficiency. The highest profile attempt at using genetic engineering for the purpose of nutritional fortification has been "golden rice." The nutritional fortification is specifically targeting vitamin A for the benefit of millions suffering from diseases related to this deficiency.

An example of a crop genetically engineered for built-in *pest resistance* is cotton. Cotton is the most pernicious crop on the planet. It grows on less than 3% of agricultural lands globally, but consumes 16% of pesticides. Cotton also requires a staggering quantity of water. (These problems are, I believe, exacerbated by attempts to grow cotton where it should not otherwise be grown.) Certainly, say defenders of genetically engineered seeds, if you care about the environment, you should love GMOs. The thought is that if the crops are genetically modified to resist insects, then the farmer doesn't have to use all of those dangerous chemicals in his or her field.

It's at this point, and with no apparent sense of irony, that GMO proponents introduce the third flavor of GMO product, the seeds that can survive direct exposure to intimidating quantities of pesticides. Although more than one company markets pesticide resistance seeds, the most prolific brand is Monsanto's Round Up Ready family of crops. As a consequence of the expanded use of Round Up Ready crops, Round Up no longer needs to be spot sprayed on weeds if the plants came from

Round Up Ready seeds; the entire field can be covered in the chemical indiscriminately.

Despite the assurances of the manufacturers that GMOs represent absolutely no risk to human health, there is a rising chorus of concern among some consumers. What follows is that consumer narrative as I see it. The opinion, interpretations, and inferences are mine and mine alone, unless otherwise attributed.

Genetically engineered seeds are often associated with the "Green Revolution" which has been credited with saving a billion humans in poor, developing countries from starvation. The GMO – Green Revolution association is a little confusing to me for two reasons. First, the Green Revolution was over by the time genetically engineered seeds came to market. Second, the Green Revolution was hardly a high-tech revolution. The Green Revolution was basically the proliferation of the chemical agriculture that had come to dominance in the United States after World War II: seeds that had been hybridized for yield when used with nitrogen fertilizer, irrigation, pesticides, and loans with which to purchase the preceding. Even 20 years ago, Gore was cynical about the ability of genetically engineered crops to breathe life into a program that had hit a glass ceiling, presciently saying in *Earth in the Balance*, "…the higher yields made possible by genetically engineered strains often cannot be sustained over time, as the pests and blights catch up to them and as overirrigation and overfertilizing take their toll on soil productivity." Regardless, crops genetically engineered for vitamin enhancement are the least controversial flavor of GMOs here in the United States; the target market for Golden Rice is Africa, not America, and the product is struggling to live up to its expectations anyway.

## The Concerns

Pest resistant and pesticide resistant crops are a different story. In the United States, they represent the overwhelming majority of any harvest (corn and soybeans in particular) for which there is a genetically engineered option. There are specific concerns for each category of crop, but a few concerns are basically the same for each. These would include the negative effects on health from the human body's inability to identify the genetically modified crop as food, which might be igniting a host of gastrointestinal and allergy-related illnesses.

*Pest resistant* crops are genetically modified to contain a protein that when eaten by an unfriendly insect, kills that pest by eating away at the insect's body from the stomach out. Manufacturers claim that the genetically inserted protein only targets the destructive pests and is not harmful to other species, including humans. There happens to be an entire ecosystem in each of our stomachs comprised of trillions of bacteria necessary for our survival. There is an understandable level of skepticism among consumers about whether or not the effect of pest resistant GMOs on this "gut flora" was ever considered, much less tested. We can follow this story right through the digestive tract. Now in the intestines, the story goes, undigested particles of genetically engineered corn and soybeans leak through the walls of the intestine and get attacked by the immune system like any other unexpected foreign object. A vicious cycle of "gut dysbiosis" (the condition of all those *good* bacteria and microorganisms in your intestinal tract being pushed out of balance by *harmful* microorganisms) and immune deregulation manifests itself in the form of allergies, asthma, and chronic illness.[40] If there is such a thing as experience-based research, it is difficult to ignore the increasingly common occurrence of allergies and asthma in children compared to three or four decades ago. It seems logical to suspect something environmental at work, and if there is one new antagonist that has touched us all in the last twenty years, it is industrial agriculture. The culprit could end up being genetically engineered crops, excessive use of antibiotics, or a toxic mix of pesticides. It could also be all of the above. Either way, consumers are starting to connect the dots.

*Pesticide resistant* crops come with all of the preceding baggage and a few proprietary concerns. Although more than one company sells seeds genetically engineered to resist herbicides, the most prolifically used is Monsanto's "Round Up Ready" family of crops. Instead of spraying only the weeds, the herbicide Round Up (in this case) can be applied indiscriminately to the entire field, killing weeds without killing the grain. The Round Up, and its active ingredient glyphosate, invades the entire plant, making its way in through the leaves down to the root tips.

Glyphosate is what is known as a "chelator." It works not by poisoning a weed, but by bonding to nutrients, making those nutrients unavailable to the plant so that it essentially dies of malnutrition or disease. Glyphosate does not need to differentiate between a weed, desirable crop, or for that matter, any other organism. In addition to worries over the risk of eating such an organism, there is a nutrition-related concern that glyphosate has the potential to make the plants susceptible to disease.[41] And that is what Dr. Don Huber, professor emeritus from Purdue University, is finding: a resurgence of plant diseases that crops with deficient immune systems cannot defend against.

I don't know if this science is irrefutable, so I lean once again on logic. I am aware of no chemical or drug that can be applied or consumed for ingestion that can be used in unlimited amounts without negative consequences. It is not true of the mighty antibiotic, or the humble aspirin. Even substances we can't live without, like salt, become poisonous at some level.

## Conclusion: We Don't Need Them

Why would we, as Americans, need these genetically modified organisms? The benefits touted are usually connected in some way to crop yields. This doesn't seem to me to be a terribly strong argument in favor of GMOs for three reasons. First, evidence of increased yields associated with new genetically engineered crops remains elusive. We are blind to the harsh truth, wrote Gore, that "the new crop varieties we create in our laboratories quickly become vulnerable to their rapidly evolving natural enemies, sometimes after only a few growing seasons. Although their genetic resistance is reinforced with new genes that are spliced into the commercial varieties every few years, many of the genes available for replenishing the vitality of food crops exist only in the wild."[42] Twenty years later, farmers are telling me to stop losing sleep over Round Up; it won't be around much longer anyway due to increasing ineffectiveness.

Secondly, as a nation (if not a world), we already produce way more calories than we need, even after scraping a third of our plate into the trashcan at the end of a meal (we're just not producing it in all the right places, leaving too much of the world hungry). Two thirds of Americans are overweight, and a third are obese. Increasingly, this is neither an American phenomenon nor is it restricted any longer to developed countries. Half of Brazilians are overweight, as are a quarter of adults in China. Obesity rates in the United States are mirrored in Mexico, Venezuela, and South Africa. Pacific Islanders and people in the Arab States of the Persian Gulf look much like us.[43]

Lastly, sustainable agriculture hasn't been standing still. The Rodale Institute recently completed a thirty-year study demonstrating similar findings to those experienced by the farmers working with Iroquois Valley Farms. After an initial decline in yields during transition, and after soil fertility has recovered, organic methods can match or surpass the results of chemical agriculture.[44] Interestingly, it seems to be especially true in times of climatic stress, such as the drought-like conditions of 2012.

The weed problem that GMOs profess to address is a direct result of monoculture, a bad idea to begin with. The claims that modifying crops genetically for pest-resistant will lead to higher yields have proven predictably elusive, for the reasons Gore feared in 1992: "when most of our crops are grown from engineered, monocultured varieties, it may be only a matter of time before predators discover a weakness in the genetic defenses of these crops for which our artificial storehouse of genes contains no remedy."[45] I think there's even a sustainable response to the chemical farming techniques used in growing cotton: grow industrial hemp or flax instead. Technological advancements in the area of textiles have reached the point where hemp and flax can be used to make a product with greater durability and tensile strength at a fraction of the cost to the environment.

The dominance of genetically modified crops presents one more area of risk to consider. It is similar to concepts in the field of ecology. One, from the study of ecological services, that argues that any species of plant or animal, no matter how seemingly trivial, is worth saving from extinction because that species might hold the key to a problem that plagues the human race, such as cancer. The other concept, and one that is a recurring theme in the study of sustainability, is that genetic diversity is a *good thing*. We genetically modify traits to be passed on from one generation to the next, to maximize yield and market value in the present day, without consideration for long-term genetic resilience. Pests and blights evolve at a constant rate, systematically searching "their own genetic arsenals for an offensive strategy that work."[46] They are no longer aiming at a moving target; each year's crop comes from just a handful of varieties instead of thousands. This genetic erosion is, according to Gore, the most serious strategic threat to the global food system.

# PART V

# Bringing It to The Table

# CHAPTER 17

# Tao Theory: Zen and the Art of Investing in Sustainable Food

## Against the Grain

Back in 2009, while pondering the coming decade of investing opportunities, I was drawn to the area of sustainability more than any other. As I spent more time drilling down into the space, I concluded that sustainable *agriculture* was the most attractive subsegment. What I didn't know was *how* one invested in sustainable agriculture. The most obvious strategy was simply to buy organic farmland.

The challenge was that I had no idea how to buy farmland of any kind (nor did I know how to farm). Within a few weeks of this mental exercise, there was a story in the *Chicago Tribune* about a guy who had formed a partnership to invest in, of all things, organic farms. Moreover, he lived just 20 miles from me. In an unusual move for an introvert, I cold called David Miller at what was then known as Working Farms Capital.

David was born in the central Illinois town of Kankakee, but he didn't grow up on a farm. Not that there wasn't farming in his blood; his second cousin is Terra Brockman, founder of The Land Connection, a nonprofit dedicated to promoting and preserving the heritage of local food production. Towards the end of a nearly thirty-year career as a corporate banker, David started to spend most of his time working on real estate transactions. This got him thinking about farmland. After dipping his toe into the water through small farm acquisitions with family members, Miller formed a partnership with his high school friend and college roommate, Dr. Steven Rivard. That partnership would eventually become Iroquois Valley Farms, the best vehicle I had seen for investing in sustainable agriculture. While Working Farms Capital was structured to accept fees for raising capital and closing on farm acquisitions, Iroquois Valley Farms was a company that would own the farms (and keep the farms organic) into perpetuity. All the other entities out there acquiring farmland (whether conventional or organic) were structured as "funds" or limited partnerships. Someday, those partnerships would sell the farms to the highest bidder, even if that meant the land would be pulled out of agriculture and developed.

After a long breakfast and some additional due diligence, I didn't just become an investor in the partnership, I got involved in helping run the company. My first job was valuing an organic farm growing cash crops: corn, soybeans, wheat, and hay. Most business appraisal work utilizes one of two methods and often both. The first method discounts the cash flow generated in the future back to the present. "Discounting" expected cash flow from the future back to the present just means that if I offered you a dollar today or a dollar tomorrow, you'd take the dollar today (a dollar today being worth more than a dollar tomorrow). So, the value today of receiving $100 a year for ten years isn't worth $1,000 ($100 x 10 years), it's worth something less than that (you want a return on your investment over time, right?).

The other method looks at the value of transactions (i.e., ownership changing hands) involving comparable companies – in other words, it looks at the price for which comparable enterprises were actually sold. This is the approach commonly used in residential real estate transactions: when you go to buy or sell a home, you look at what similar homes in the area have sold for in order to figure out what the home you are valuing is worth. It is also the most common approach used to value farmland.

As an investor valuing operating companies, I had always discounted future expected cash flow to estimate worth. It's superior to the other methods because discounting forecasted cash flow takes into consideration how different every business is in reality. In valuing industrial farms (i.e., those conventionally farmed), there is little variation in technique, inputs, or crops (which are literally and figuratively commodities), and every farmer plays to the same set of subsidies. Therefore, those farms were simply appraised based on the prices of farms that had sold nearby (assumed to have similar soil quality and yield potential) in the recent past – they were treated like any other form of real estate. And that method makes sense for conventional farmland producing a commodity product. No one that I had been able to find had ever built a model that looked at a farm as a business, or operating company. I believe this is because no one had ever considered organic farming to be a substantially different, and more importantly, *better* business than conventional farming. This is going to change, and it will be an important step in getting people to believe that sustainable agriculture can in fact feed the world. But I digress.

Forget about the results of that first individual analysis, the one of the organic farm. It was the exercise itself that was so enlightening. I sat down with a farm consultant and walked through all the inputs, primarily seeds, manure, and labor. This farm had been used in conventional agriculture for at least a generation. It would need to be "transitioned" to certified organic land. The first three years of that transition period (i.e., the three years the farm must be unsullied by chemicals to receive certified organic status) are tough on the business. Yields drop in the first year without chemical inputs because the soil is devoid of nutrients necessary to support plant growth, and yet you are still selling crops at lower (than organic), conventional prices. Fertility improves each year, and then after the transition to organic, prices for the crops improve dramatically. The farmer would be using a four-year rotation in this case, which means that the farm would be divided into four fields of approximately equal size. Each year, one field would be seeded in corn, one in soybeans, one in wheat, and one in a legume that would not be harvested. Changing the crop grown on a particular piece of land helps the farmer keep the pests (weeds and insects) guessing. That last part of the rotation, the legume, is the fertility-building year. Plants in the legume family are used to "fix" nitrogen, or put nitrogen back into the soil. This is a critical process used by organic farmers to fertilize or add fertility to the soil (in the absence of chemical fertilizer use). That crop is not harvested, but plowed back into the soil to further enhance fertility. Plowing that fourth of the farm under, however, was a real drag on cash flow compared to a conventional farm model. I wasn't sure this sustainable agriculture model would ever be competitive with industrial agriculture. That was, until we got to the expense side of the ledger.

In my prior life, I had owned shares in one of the publicly traded fertilizer companies, so I understood the "bullish case" for fertilizer from the perspective of the chemical companies: A billion or so people in Asia were moving to the middle class and would switch from a rice diet to a protein diet (i.e., a diet with more meat), generating rising demand for the grains to feed livestock and therefore the inputs of chemical agriculture that made monoculture grain-growing viable on a massive scale. At the time I met with the fertilizer manufacturer, the company was forecasting that the United States would become an exporter of corn to China in the following year. The future was bright.

Back in Illinois, as I tried to put a value on the organic farm, the light bulb went on. The chemical companies' gain was the farmers' pain. The chemical inputs of nitrogen, phosphorous, and potassium were all either directly or indirectly tied to natural resources that would become increasingly scarce and expensive over time, but farmers had to have them to succeed in conventional agriculture. Moreover, industrial farmers buy seed from a monopoly. The two things that an industrial farmer or farm investor could say for sure were that they had no control over their costs, and their costs were going higher. Farm subsidies are often criticized for being a gift to large corporate farms. They would be more accurately described as a subsidy to the chemical companies and the industrial buyers of the grains (food processors). The conventional farmer, big or small, is getting little more than his costs reimbursed over a lifetime of work.

The sustainable farmer doesn't have the same exposure to cost pressure. After the sun itself, manure is the ultimate renewable resource, replacing the increasingly costly fertilizers. Yet, because I believed in the secular trend towards organic food, the sustainable farmer would continue to benefit from rising market prices for organic crops (in this example, organic grains) over time. I was concluding that not only was sustainable farming a good business and investment, but it was a better investment than industrial farmland. (Compound the cost pressures faced by industrial agriculture with the fact that forty percent of the domestic corn crop was going to ethanol, itself an industry that only exists because of regulatory favoritism towards agribusiness, and I wasn't sure I wanted *any* exposure to non-organic farmland.)

Aside from the appeal of organic farmland as an investment class, I liked some of the innovations David had brought to the market for sustainable farmland investing. First among them was a long-term lease to the sustainable farmer. Conventional leases (for farmers who don't own the land they are cultivating, known as tenant farmers) last for one year at a time. Basically, there was no commitment between landowner and farmer beyond the next harvest. The farmer's only motivation then is to extract as much value as possible from the soil in the current year. Sustainable agriculture, with its approach toward building fertility in the soil instead of just drawing it down, requires a different approach. There are going to be years where the best thing to do with that subpar soybean crop is to plow it under and get the benefit from better fertility and higher yield in the following year. Long-term leases diminish the incentive to take one too many cuttings of hay, lest the root system that fixes nitrogen in the soil gets too shallow. A five to seven year lease gives the farmer the ability to benefit from managing with a long-term view towards better fertility and higher yields.

The second innovation was a lease structure that puts farmer and landowner in the same boat. A nominal fixed rent per acre covers the cost of any debt service incurred in the acquisition of the land. Beyond that, the farmer has a chance to earn a respectable living, and in exceptional years, both farmer and landowner share in the bounty. Note that David's innovative lease structure benefits both the farmer and the investor.

Add one more advantage to sustainable agriculture in the battle for investment dollars: Fertile soils hold water better during periods of drought. This was the theory, and the summer of 2012 provided the first support. In the regions where they operated, our transitioned farms outperformed "conventional" yields in the toughest conditions since the Dust Bowl.

I admit to taking solace whenever someone infinitely smarter than me shares my perspective. In July 2012, Jeremy Grantham (the Grantham in Grantham, Mayo, Van Otterloo & Company, LLC, a global investment firm managing over $100 billion) published a quarterly letter to clients that summarizes what he considers to be the beginnings of a severe, long-term global food crisis. In the report, Grantham documents declines in grain productivity despite staggering increases in fertilizer use. He talks about degradation of farmland due to poor agricultural practices, "which will continue to undermine our long-term sustainable productive capacity." Moreover, he provides support for the view that the input costs of chemical agriculture, based as they are upon natural resource extraction, will rise to very painful levels. All of this is set against a backdrop of dwindling fresh water, rising world population, and climate change. Organic farming is a solution that requires merely brains and will, not extraordinary technological innovations or massive capital investments. The investment implication, he concludes, is that natural resources should represent 30% of a long-term portfolio, with farming and forestry at the top of the list. And sustainable agriculture is the only form of agriculture that will endure. So tying it all together, the investment case for agriculture generally is strong, and the case for sustainable agriculture is stronger still. In my opinion, Iroquois Valley Farms is the most compelling investment model within the sustainable agriculture sector.

Iroquois Valley Farms has been built entirely on individual investors up to this point. It has been difficult to get institutions (endowments, trusts, private equity funds, etc.), interested in the company because of its small size and the illiquid (the shares in the company do not trade freely on any exchange) nature of the investment. Many institutions have so much money (and consider it imprudent to be more than a small percentage owner in any individual investment) they are mathematically precluded from investing in a company as small as IVF. Moreover, the institutions want to see an "exit strategy" for their investment, i.e., a way to sell the investment at a time of their choosing.

There is generally one other hurdle that some institutions claim keeps them from getting excited about sustainable agriculture as an asset class. Currently, they say, organic farmland doesn't sell at any premium to "conventional" farmland. So far, they are absolutely right. But isn't that the arbitrage? Isn't that an opportunity to take advantage of two dissimilar assets being valued at the same price? How is it that if you put two acres of land next to each other, and one is lifeless and sullied by chemicals while the other is clean and teaming with life, that the latter is not worth more than the former? The institutional investors are saying that for an organic farm to be worth more than a conventional farm, the organic farm has to generate more free cash flow. That's a high hurdle in a market with such significant externalities, but it is also true. The analysis I walked through in 2010 convinced me that an organic farm would, in fact, generate more cash over the long-term than a conventional farm for just the reasons that Grantham pointed out in his quarterly letter to clients. We have already reached a point where conventional agriculture requires more chemical inputs to keep yields flat. In Grantham's view, we are reaching a point where we actually go backwards; despite more chemical inputs, yields will decline. However, it's true that it's difficult to see sustainable farming's competitive strengths in what little published research is out there. There just aren't a lot of meaningful data points. The modern organic farming universe is still young and tiny, and the analyses comparing conventional practices fine-tuned over decades to the trial and error methods of sustainable agriculture are unfair (as is cherry-picking results from the best organic farms).

Another issue is the difference in prices between conventional and organic products. Will organic prices come down? I believe the spread between conventional and organic will close, but due more to "conventional" prices rising to close the gap than organic prices falling. Right now the premium for organic food is as high as it is in part because demand exceeds supply. There does need to be a premium, however, for basic financial reasons. An organic farm in transition needs to look at higher prices in the future to compensate for the three years of dilution caused by the transition to organic. This much is basic. It is also important for a premium to exist so the market for sustainable farming attracts investment capital and new farmers. The 55-year-old farmer who has spent a lifetime farming with the way our system of subsidies incents the farmer to practice is not going to see the return in switching to organic methods this late in life. It is the young beginning farmer, usually lacking in sufficient savings to buy the first 80 acres, who holds the key.

And in fact, the premium *is* attracting young farmers. When I asked one of Iroquois Valley's new young farmers why he was switching to organic methods, he sheepishly shrugged and said, "Because I'll make more money." Rather than be offended that he wasn't focused on the environmental or societal benefits, I was elated, not because he wanted to make more, but because he believed he *would* make more money. Scott Friedman, a farmer who has been with Iroquois Valley longer than any other, told me the same thing in 2010 about his personal conversion to organic methods. This is validation. If we want more good food to eat, we need more smart, hard-working people to get into sustainable agriculture. Grantham is more specific: we need farmers who are willing to work longer hours and a longer year. To attract more high-quality people, these individuals need to be able to make more money.

## Impact Investing

This isn't your father's socially responsible investing. "Socially responsible investing" was always about avoiding companies with products or services that were perceived to have a negative impact on society, such as cigarettes, guns, casinos, and alcohol. In the vernacular of the portfolio manager, excluding such industries during the construction of a portfolio is referred to as a "negative screen." By getting involved with Iroquois Valley Farms, I unintentionally walked in to the field of "Impact Investing." Impact Investing isn't about *avoiding* a negative social impact; it's about generating a positive financial return while having an additional positive return to society as a natural consequence of a company's activities. Make no mistake, I felt in 2009, and do now, that sustainable agriculture is superior to most other available asset classes based purely on the relative returns it offers. However, as an environmental advocate and father to young children, I personally understand and value the other benefits to society created by organic agriculture. Funds, trusts, and endowments looking for both investment returns and "impact" should find sustainable farmland compelling for the same reasons.

There are two flavors within the category of Impact Investing. The first flavor emphasizes economic return over social return, while the second emphasizes social return over economic return. Sustainable agriculture, because of its favorable outlook, fits neatly into the first category, however, it also possesses characteristics that make the social benefits as significant as any other initiatives out there.

I don't know how long the term "Impact Investing" will be around and relevant. If climate change is for real, if we are entering a period of permanently increasing natural resource scarcity, and if the "green revolution" is over while population growth isn't, then things like sustainable agriculture or alternative energy need no longer be viewed solely in the context of social benefit, tangible or intangible. It may be a function purely of outright societal need. In the mean time, the beneficiaries or targets of impact investment dollars must speak to something like the "triple bottom line" as defined by Iroquois Valley Farms: solid financial performance, human and environmental health concerns, and fostering community through small family farms.

## Micro-Lending

While sustainable food appeared to me to be the sector with the best secular growth prospects back in 2009, the best pure *financial* opportunity was in making loans. In the years following the economic meltdown of the last decade, banking, specifically making loans, should have been a great business. That is except that banks didn't seem to be making loans, even though there were great loans to be made.

Some of the best lending opportunities I was seeing at the time were admittedly tiny and unusual in nature. Much has been written about the enormous social benefit that has come from making very small loans on market terms (not charity) in developing countries. Sometimes what stands between having an entrepreneurial ambition and seeing the idea become reality is just a few thousand or even hundreds of dollars. But that's not just true in India. It's also true right here, and it's especially true in the sustainable food business.

As mentioned earlier, the grass-fed beef business has a very high return on investment, but it is very demanding from a working capital perspective. Cliff McConville had the opportunity to get in to the beef business with twelve six-month old beeves, but needed about $1,000 a head to acquire them. No traditional lender was interested (or, in their defense, no traditional lender had a history with making such loans, and therefore didn't know how to underwrite, or calculate an appropriate interest rate on, the loan). Knowing Cliff personally (Barrington Natural Farms was my organic feed delivery company's first "commercial" customer), knowing what I knew about the demand for this product, and knowing that customers were willing to put down deposits, I jumped at the chance to loan Cliff the money myself. There was simply no better risk-adjusted return opportunity available to me at that time (when banks were offering less than 1% on deposits), and the money would stay and be recycled in the community.

I'm not the first person to talk about this kind of lending. Author Michael Shuman wrote an entire book on this subject of investing locally, called *Local Dollars, Local Sense*. The book covers the normal but somewhat forgotten network of small community banks and credit unions that should be taking first crack at this microloan market. Even for them, however, loans under $50,000 might be considered uneconomic. Not only does nearly as much work goes in to making a small loan as a large loan, but the banks have no lending history to lean on when doing credit analysis on things like beef cattle. The bank can't look at thousands or millions of examples of loans to small cheese makers to determine the likelihood of being paid back. And if the bank weren't paid back, what the bank would do with the kitchen equipment (the security on the loan)? Contrast this with a car loan. The loan itself is likely even smaller than $50,000, but the bank has decades of lending history (on cars) with which to analyze that loan (i.e., the analysis is much easier and less time consuming). More importantly, if the bank has to repossess that car, it knows there is a ready secondary market for used cars. So, if a bank is going to make a loan to a business or secured by an asset it has never been involved with before, a lot of work is required and that extra work is tough to justify on a small loan.

Out of necessity, Schuman also covers the web of SEC regulations haunting any attempt to sell shares or interests in a fund or partnership. In the overwhelming majority of cases, those partnerships are looking to own a percentage of your company through an equity investment (inherently more regulated), and a majority of the opportunities are only available to accredited investors, or folks who already have a high net worth or high income. I am more interested in seeing individuals fill the niche left open by the banking community: More loans will get made, more individuals will "connect" with their local food sources, and community will be strengthened.

For all the reasons already mentioned (administrative costs, lack of experience with a particular form of loan security, etc), most banks, big or small, simply won't be able to justify loaning a local farmer $10,000 secured by Black Angus. I can, however, and so can you. Even if $10,000 is more than you can prudently lend to a single borrower, imagine the equivalent of an investment club that lends to local businesses instead of investing in the stock market. I admit that I have insight into "Cliff The Borrower" that a bank is unlikely to have. But isn't that the point? If you are comparing the risk associated with investing in something a thousand miles away or in someone you've never met, compared to the farmer who is producing beef that you yourself would eat, which looks like the safer bet?

The risk associated with a smaller, and by definition, simpler story to understand, favors the smaller loan. If done in a group instead of individually, prudence requires that you still check with both SEC regulations and regulations in your state. But it's definitely worth the time. If a food entrepreneur is funding a business with credit cards that charge double-digit interest rates, and you are earning next to zero on your money market account and certificates of deposit at the local bank, there is a *lot* of room in between for both parties to do better. As the lender, you're not only making a loan available, you're making the loan *affordable*.[47]

The subject of financing a sustainable food business is complex and ever changing, especially on the regulatory front. Justice simply cannot be done to the topic in a single chapter, no less a few paragraphs. If you are serious about seeking financing for your sustainable food venture, I recommend reading a book or two dedicated to the subject. *Raising Dough: The Complete Guide to Financing a Socially Responsible Food Business* is both the most recent update on the topic as well as one narrowly focused on the sustainable food space. Don't leave home without it.

# CHAPTER 18

# A Cooperative Polyculture

## The Farm

Going back to the story of Cliff McConville violating one of Joel Salatin's ten markers for success (by starting too many new ventures at once) got me thinking. Maybe Joel Salatin is one in a million, and maybe Cliff isn't far behind. There probably aren't a lot of people who, even with a decade head start, could grow all the plants and raise all the animals that the local market desires. Nor should anyone need to try.

The word "polyculture," in its most general usage, refers to a system of agriculture designed to mimic natural ecosystems, specifically through the diversity of species. Growing multiple species of plants in the same space is often described as "polyculture," but I think that usage dilutes the concept; plants don't exist in nature in the absence of animals. Barrington Natural Farms leased additional acreage for pasturing cattle and broilers, but the land was still underutilized. Enter Natasha Leigh, another young farmer with a few milking goats in need of pasture. At the age of 21, and with no more upfront capital than the cost of the goats, Natasha is in business. Maybe Jeff Leider of JL Honey puts a few hives on the perimeter, and another farmer adds hogs to the wooded acres that is part of Barrington Natural Farms' lease but isn't being utilized. Now imagine that an entity such as Iroquois Valley Farms, with its network of accredited investors, comes in and buys that land so it will always be organic and available (through a long-term lease to Barrington Natural Farms); another cycle is completed, another loop closed. This is the outdoor version of a "cooperative polyculture." With different "species" of plants, animals, and end products, the same concept could be accomplished indoors. That model has its own name: the vertical farm.

# The Plant

Nearly 150 years ago, a group of nine railroad companies acquired swampland on the south side of Chicago in order to consolidate the disparate stockyards around the city. This area became known as the Union Stockyards, or simply, The Yards. At its peak, nearly 10 million animals were butchered in a year at The Yards and processed at neighboring meatpacking facilities. Slaughterhouses and meatpackers deliberately set up on the banks of the Chicago River or its branches.[48] Staggering amounts of water were pumped from the Chicago River in to The Yards to facilitate the processing, and an equally staggering amount of waste was pumped back in to the river. Worried about contaminating Lake Michigan and therefore Chicago's drinking water, engineers reversed the flow of the Chicago River, sending the slurry out towards the Mississippi. In his book *The Jungle*, Upton Sinclair described a world where two hundred and fifty miles of track...

> "brought about ten thousand head of cattle every day, and as many hogs, and half as many sheep – which meant some eight or ten million live creatures turned into food every year...There were groups of cattle being driven to the chutes, which were roadways about fifteen feet wide, raised high above the pens. In these chutes the stream of animals was continuous; it was uncanny to watch them, pressing on to their fate, all unsuspicious – a very river of death."

This muckraking story about the inhumanity of working life in The Union Stockyards led to the passage of the Pure Food and Drug Act. Eventually, the railroads' growing reach allowed livestock to be processed closer to the farm, making this version of the concentrated system temporarily obsolete. The concentrated system would return, of course, if not in one geographic location, in still massive facilities dispersed throughout the country but still controlled by less than a handful of corporations. That is the system that remains in place today.

The residential neighborhood around The Yards, known as The Back of the Yards, is still bound by iron. Located directly on one of those old rail lines, in one of the last meatpacking facilities held over from the days when Chicago was "hog butcher to the world," a new kind of food production system is taking root. In a four-story building abandoned in 2006 by a processing company called Peer Foods, an industrial real estate developer and his team are constructing a "vertical farm" called The Plant. The nearly 100,000 square foot building is still primarily a shell, but by 2017, it is expected to be a model of large-scale urban agriculture and food production for all of the world to see.

Once completed, The Plant's tenants will include a bakery and a kombucha tea brewery. The facility will also contain a commercial kitchen, following the way blazed by Alexis Leverenz and Zina Murray, which will enable dozens of other food startups to lease space by the hour. The first food to leave The Plant for market came from The Plant's own aquaponics system in the basement of the building. Run by The Plant's Farm Manager, Carla McGarrah, the aquaponics system is a microcosm of what The Plant aspires to be: a closed-loop system. Waste product from one stop on the loop is utilized somewhere else. Once functional, little enters besides people, or leaves the loop, except food.

Aquaponics is the combination of hydroponics, growing plants in a soilless medium (water), and aquaculture, which means raising fish in tanks. The waste stream produced by the fish flows downhill to a shallow pool where plants float in foam beds like lily pads, roots dangling underwater. The plants utilize the nutrients in the fish waste as fertilizer, simultaneously cleaning the water for its return to the fish tanks. Like the farmer in the Gene Logsdon story who is raising cattle just for the value of the manure, the fish (tilapia in this case) are there primarily to provide the fertilizer. Though they will be harvested eventually, the fish might only fetch a few dollars a pound. The leafy greens, grown in the nutrient rich water provided by the fish tanks, will sell for around $50 a pound. This can be done year round. Restaurants are falling over themselves to get Carla's leafy greens, but she sells out every week at the Logan Square Farmers Market.

Even in a well-insulated building such as The Plant, growing plants indoors requires a lot of energy. The solution to the energy challenge at The Plant is beer, or more specifically, a microbrewery. Beer, said Benjamin Franklin, is living proof that God loves us and wants us to be happy. Though the USDA doesn't recognize "beer" as one of the major food groups, microbreweries are still pioneers in the local food movement. Since bottoming at less than 100 in the late 1970's, the number of breweries in the United States has exploded to over 2000.[49] (Evidently, it's easier to get people to spend a little more on good beer than it is to get them to spend a little more on good burgers and broccoli.) The act of transporting beer, like any liquid, produces a high "carbon footprint" – it's expensive and takes a lot of fuel. Doing the brewing and consuming in-region is very environmentally friendly.

The brewing process does create a fair bit of waste, however, called "brewers mash," or spent grains. That waste stream can be utilized at The Plant for the on-site generation of electricity and heat. Generating its own power is one way The Plant becomes both environmentally viable *and* financially viable. The brewers mash (and other food waste) will be fed into an "anaerobic digester," which can convert the waste into a gas that when burned will run a generator deep in the bowels of the building. Anaerobic digestion works something like a mechanical stomach or a compost pile. Through a combination of microscopic bugs and high heat, the brewers waste will essentially be composted in just 30 days from start to finish, a fraction of the time it would take if left to nature. Anaerobic digestion isn't a new technology. One engineer in the field told me that the first anaerobic digesters were used 150 years ago in a leper colony in India. Different versions of the technology are being used on livestock operations around the world to process manure. The negative aspect of the livestock model is that the anaerobic digester is necessarily associated with a confined animal feeding operation (how else could you collect the manure). The microbrewery, in contrast, is an environmentally friendly way to produce beer *and* power.

The scope of this project is huge. The Plant's building would be prohibitively expensive to construct from scratch. The visionary architect of The Plant, John Edel, purchased the building for less than $6 a square foot. Anyone else would have torn the building down, sold the scrap, and built a brand new building. Instead, Edel and his team are using the thick, well-insulated (and food grade) building as a low-cost way to take the vertical farm concept from drawing board to reality. It is a completely different business plan for a vertical farm than the glass-walled skyscrapers envisioned by academics. Those structures would be too expensive for the low-margin food business.[50]

The plan is ambitious, but there are plenty of reasons for optimism. For starters, Edel has accomplished something similar once already. An industrial designer by education, he left a career in broadcast television design with the skills to build seemingly anything he could dream up, and without spending a lot of money. Through his for-profit company, Bubbly Dynamics, Edel acquired an empty paint factory in 2002 and transformed it into a profitable small-business incubator called the Chicago Sustainable Manufacturing Center. In both cases, he lowered the business risk by buying at a fire-sale price, reusing the majority of the materials left on site, and funding the plan personally instead of depending on big bank loans.

Like anything with great potential, The Plant's business plan is not without risk. The power generation is key to both its environmental and financial viability. The microbrewery is an important piece of the puzzle, and the first brewery tenant slotted for the space backed out at the eleventh hour. The wood-burning oven in the bakery is another large, single-purpose investment. Similar to any ecosystem that depends on the health of the microorganisms within it, the success of The Plant will be dependent on the success of its "manufacturing" tenants.

Though food production is the goal, the project is about keeping costs down and closing loops. The cheapest building is the reused building; in the case of The Plant, it's also the greenest. Edel looks forward to sharing a successful vertical farm model with the world so that other derelict buildings can be converted for productive use. Is The Plant's model replicable? In the U.S., there is no shortage of derelict buildings, which quickly become a social liability. Reusing those structures for urban agriculture turns a net negative in to a positive. I don't know how many abandoned buildings are, like The Plant's, already up to USDA standards (which makes meeting FDA standards relatively easy). No doubt, every project will be different. As long as people with the winning combination of Edel's contracting skills and creativity are willing to roll up their sleeves, anything is possible.

# CHAPTER 19

# Opt Out

The current transformation, wrote John Ikerd, is being driven by questions of sustainability: How can we meet the needs of the present without diminishing opportunities for the future? I believe we are at a critical juncture. As a society, we are simultaneously at breaking points in the realms of personal health, ecological health, and financial health. The time to act is now. We must start "doing." Despite the confluence of crises, I am hopeful. It would be difficult not to be inspired and hopeful after meeting the local food advocates in this story. I'm further biased by the knowledge that there are a hundred other equally inspiring stories I didn't get to tell. And that's just in my region of the world.

There are always sources of pessimism; in between the start and finish of this manuscript, Chicagoland lost two restaurants that served only sustainable fare. Market forces are as relentless as the tide. The good news is that even in the face of intimidating odds, people are starting to act. The numbers are still small, and setbacks intrude every day, but there is finally momentum. The path toward a sustainable food system is a difficult one. Higher callings always seem to require more work: jazz, aikido, dry-fly fishing. Organic farming is no different.

I hope more people are moved to answer the call to join the local food movement. I hope people see the availability of good food as a form of sovereignty, as important as ownership of land or possession of civil rights. Among the collection of essays from which the title of this section is named, Wendell Berry writes, "We still (sometimes) remember that we cannot be free if our minds and voices are controlled by someone else. But we neglected to understand that we cannot be free if our food and its sources are controlled by someone else. The condition of the passive consumer of food is not a democratic condition. One reason to eat responsibly is to live free."[51] That quote comes from an essay entitled "The Pleasures of Eating," and at a minimum, I hope more people are inspired to experience the joy of sustainable food. I hope the reader further understands that no one needs to eat exotic grains and berries from remote South American villages in order to be healthy or happy. Just eat local food that tastes as nature intended it to taste, and you will be nourished, body and soul. Lastly, I hope beyond hope that someone somewhere figures out *something* to do with the *rest* of the quinoa.

# Acknowledgements

How do you thank people without in any way implicating them in the work they inspired but shouldn't be held responsible for? Such is the challenge of the first time, amateur author. Neva Knott, Lauren Imlay, and Beth Hanratty Fields, thank you for everything. Thanks to Maria Rodriguez, former Long Grove Village President. Thank you to everyone that agreed to be interviewed for this book. A huge thank you to the supporters of this book's Kickstarter campaign, Cliff McConville of Barrington Natural Farms, Randall Wernes, Glenn Weidlich, Deborah Hach Bria, and my brother in the fire service, Steve Raibick. A special thanks to Dan O'Brien for "the phone call that kept me from quitting." Last but not least, thank you to my wife Krista for putting up with me during this process.

# About The Author

John Emrich brings a fresh, well-rounded perspective to his debut title, The Local Yolk. Through his education, career, and daily life, he has accumulated extensive experience and knowledge that make him uniquely qualified to write on the local food movement from both a professional and personal standpoint.

Emrich holds master's degrees in business and environmental studies, and has twenty-five years of investment and corporate finance experience. Not afraid to get his white collar a little soiled, he left the corporate world in 2010 to found Backyard Chicken Run, a delivery service focused on helping the urban homesteader establish and maintain a sustainable living. He also helps the sustainable food movement as a board member of Iroquois Valley Farms LLC, which, among its other endeavors, backs organic farming efforts by buying farms and leasing them back to farmers who couldn't otherwise afford to keep them running.

You can learn more and continue the discussion at www.thelocalyolkbook.com.

# End Notes

[1] Tolle, Eckhart. *A New Earth: Awakening to Your Life's Purpose* (New York: Plume Publishing, 2005, p. 274).

[2] Ikerd, John. *The Essentials of Economic Sustainability* (Sterling, VA: Kumarian Press, 2012, p. 19).

[3] Schumacher, E.F. *Small is Beautiful: Economics as if People Mattered* (New York: Harper & Row Publishers, 1973).

Chapter 1

[4] Halweil, Brian. *Home Grown: The Case For Local Food In A Global Market.* (Worldwatch Paper 163, November 2002).

[5] Mother Earth News. Retrieved from: http://www.motherearthnews.com/Real-Food/2007-10-01/Tests-Reveal-Healthier-Eggs.aspx

[6] Soil and Health. Retrieved from: http://www.soilandhealth.org/06clipfile/0601.LEMag/LE%20Magazine%2C%20March%202001%20-%20Report%20Vegetables%20Without%20Vitamins.htm

[7] The Center For Food Safety. Retrieved from: http://www.centerforfoodsafety.org/pubs/USDA%20NASS%20Backgrounder-FINAL.pdf

Chapter 2

[8] USDA. Retrieved from: http://www.fsis.usda.gov/Factsheets/Egg_Products_and_Food_Safety/index.asp#13

[9] Center for Disease Control. Retrieved from: http://www.cdc.gov/HomeandRecreationalSafety/images/dogbreeds-a.pdf

Chapter 4

[10] Brand, Stewart. *Whole Earth Discipline: An Ecopragmatist Manifesto* (New York: Penguin Group, 2009, p. 51).


Chapter 5

[11] Cronon, William. *Nature's Metropolis: Chicago and the Great West* (New York: Norton & Company, 1991, p. 283).
[12] McGinnis, Michael Vincent. *Bioregionalism* (New York: Routledge, 1999).


Chapter 6

[13] Flottum, Kim. *The Backyard Beekeeper* (Beverly, MA: Quarry Books, 2005, 2010, p. 24).
[14] Jacobsen, Rowan. *Fruitless Fall: The Collapse of the Honey Bee and the Coming Agricultural Crisis* (New York: Bloomsbury, 2008, p. 63).
[15] Jacobsen, Rowan. *Fruitless Fall: The Collapse of the Honey Bee and the Coming Agricultural Crisis* (New York: Bloomsbury, 2008, pp. 98-164).
[16] Jacobsen, Rowan. *Fruitless Fall: The Collapse of the Honey Bee and the Coming Agricultural Crisis* (New York: Bloomsbury, 2008).
[17] Flottum, Kim. *The Backyard Beekeeper* (Beverly, MA: Quarry Books, 2005, 2010).
[18] Flottum, Kim. *The Backyard Beekeeper* (Beverly, MA: Quarry Books, 2005, 2010).
[19] Style, Sue. *Honey From Hive to Honey Pot* (San Francisco: Chronicle Books, 1993).
[20] Flottum, Kim. *The Backyard Beekeeper* (Beverly, MA: Quarry Books, 2005, 2010).
[21] Buchman, Stephen. *Letters from the Hive: An Intimate History of Bees, Honey, and Humankind* (New York: Bantom Dell, 2005).
[22] Jacobsen, Rowan. *Fruitless Fall: The Collapse of the Honey Bee and the Coming Agricultural Crisis* (New York: Bloomsbury, 2008).
[23] Malcom, Stanford T., and Bonney, Richard E. *Storey's Guide to Keeping Honey Bees* (North Adams, MA: Storey Publishing, 2010).
[24] Kessler, Brad. *Goat Song: A Seasonal Life, A Short History of Herding, and the Art of Making Cheese* (New York: Scribner, 2009, p. 164).

Chapter 7

[25] Nestle, Marion. *Food Politics: How the Food Industry Influences Nutrition and Health* (Berkeley, CA: University of California Press, 2002, 2007).

Chapter 8

[26] Dunn, Rob. *The Wild Life Of Our Bodies: Predators, Parasites, and Partners That Shape Who We Are Today* (New York: HarperCollins, 2011).
[27] Gumpert, David E. *Raw Milk Revolution: Behind America's Emerging Battle Over Food Rights* (White River Junction, VT: Chelsea Green Publishing, 2009, p. 43).
[28] Kessler, Brad. *Goat Song: A Seasonal Life, A Short History of Herding, and the Art of Making Cheese* (New York: Scribner, 2009, p. 157).

Chapter 9

[29] McNamee, Thomas. *Alice Waters and Chez Panisse* (New York: Penguin Press, 2007).

Chapter 13

[30] Zivan, David. "Somebody Give This Guy a Genius Grant," *Chicago Magazine*. Retrieved from: http://www.chicagomag.com/Chicago-Magazine/September-2004/Somebody-Give-This-Guy-a-Genius-Grant/
[31] Logsdon, Gene. *Holy Shit: Managing Manure to Save Mankind* (White River Junction, VT: Chelsea Green Publishing, 2010, p. 8)
[32] Howard, Louise E. *Sir Albert Howard in India* (Emmaus, Pa.: Rodale Press, 1954, p. 162).
[33] MacDonald, Christine. *Green Inc.* (Guildford, CT: The Lyons Press, 2008).
[34] Tuchman, Barbara. *The March of Folly: From Troy to Vietnam* (New York: Ballantine Books, 1984).
[35] O'Brien, Dan. *Buffalo for the Broken Heart* (New York: Random House, 2002, pp. 81-82).

Chapter 15

[36] Richardson, Jill. *Recipe For America* (Brooklyn, NY: Ig Publishing, 2009).

[37] Lustig, Dr. Robert. *Fat Chance: Beating the Odds Against Sugar, Processed Food, Obesity, and* Disease (New York: Hudson Street Pres, 2013, p. 155).

[38] Wallach, Dr. Joel D., and Lan, Dr. Ma. *Dead Doctors Don't Lie* (Bonita, CA: Wellness Publications, 1999).

Chapter 16

[39] Gore, Al. *Earth In the Balance: Ecology and the Human Spirit* (New York: First Plume Printing, 1993).

[40] Lambert, Beth. *A Compromised Generation: The Epidemic of Chronic Illness in America's Children* (Boulder, CO: First Sentient Publications, 2010).

[41] Johal, G.S., and Huber, D.M. "Glyphosate effects on disease of plants." *European Journal of Agronomy*, 31 (2009): 144-152. Retrieved from: http://www.organicconsumers.org/documents/huber-glyphosates-2009.pdf

[42] Gore, Al. *Earth In the Balance: Ecology and the Human Spirit* (New York: First Plume Printing, 1993, p. 129).

[43] "Fat Chance." *The Economist*, December 15th – 21st, 2012, Volume 405 Number 8815, pg. 15-16.

[44] Rodale Institute. Retrieved from: http://rodaleinstitute.org/our-work/farming-systems-trial/

[45] Gore, Al. *Earth In the Balance: Ecology and the Human Spirit* (New York: First Plume Printing, 1993, p. 131).

[46] Gore, Al. *Earth In the Balance: Ecology and the Human Spirit* (New York: First Plume Printing, 1993, p. 129)

Chapter 17

[47] Shuman, Michael. *Local Dollars, Local Sense: How to Shift Your Money from Wall Street to Main Street and Achieve Real Prosperity* (White River Junction, VT: Chelsea Green Publishing, 2012).

# END NOTES

Chapter 18

[48] Wade, Louise Carroll. *Chicago's Pride: The Stockyards, Packingtown, and Environs in the Nineteenth Century* (Urbana and Chicago: University of Illinois Press, 1987).
[49] Brewers Association. Retrieved from: http://www.brewersassociation.org/pages/business-tools/craft-brewing-statistics/number-of-breweries
[50] Cockrall-King, J. "An Inside Job," *Conservation*, Summer 2012, Volume 13, Number 2, pp. 31-37).

Chapter 18

[51] Berry, Wendell. *Bringing it to the Table: On Farming and Food* (Berkeley, CA: Counterpoint, 2009, p. 229)

36923743R00110

Made in the USA
Charleston, SC
20 December 2014